San Francisco

DIRECTIONS

WRITTEN AND RESEARCHED BY

Mark Ellwood

NEW YORK • LONDON • DELHI

www.roughguides.com

Contents

Introduction to San Francisco

One of America's most beautiful cities, San Francisco sits on a fog-capped, hilly peninsula bounded by the shimmering waters of San Francisco Bay to the east and the crashing waves of the Pacific Ocean to the west. Whether you're drawn in by the natural setting, or the free-spirited, nonconformist ways for which the city is also famous, you'll find plenty to keep you occupied once there.

The steep streets are lined with picturesque rows of Victorian houses, and the neighborhoods running alongside dotted with sophisticated restaurants, and chic clubs occupying converted warehouses. What's more, there's an almost small town feel to it all – provided you don't mind the hills, nearly every major sight is just a walk or short bike ride away, and if you do, a great old cable car system provides an equally fun way of getting around.

When to visit

San Francisco's climate is among the most stable in the world, with a daytime temperature that rarely ventures more than 5ºF either side of 60ºF (15ºC) but can drop much lower at night. Summer does offer some sunny days of course, but it also sees heavy fog roll in through the Golden Gate to smother the city. Winters bring most of the city's rainfall, sometimes in quite torrential storms. The nicest times to visit are **late May** and **June**, when the hills are greenest and covered with wildflowers, or **October** and **November**, when you can be fairly sure of good weather and reduced crowds at the major attractions.

▸ North Beach

Named for St Francis of Assisi, the city was transformed almost overnight in the 1840s from a sleepy fishing village to a Gold Rush boomtown. The hilly terrain didn't daunt the prospectors who threw up a city here, and the cataclysmic earthquakes and fires (most notably in 1906 and 1989) only seemed to make people more determined to stay.

Those hills have since helped define the city, both by wealth – in general, the higher up you are, the better the views and the bigger the rents – and geography, serving to divide up the dense cluster of districts in

▸ Lombard Street

Alamo Square

the northeast corner. Much of the best streetlife is experienced either around here or in iconic, energetic neighborhoods like the Mission, the Castro, and the Haight, smack in the center of the peninsula. Things open up considerably as you move north and west, to expansive parklands and beaches, and lesser-known residential areas in which you can easily stumble across some of the best ethnic food in the city.

The rest of the Bay Area is quite varied and offers a good complement to cultured city life. Cross the Golden Gate Bridge north to the rocky Marin Headlands and undisturbed Muir Woods for a fine natural escape; further on, the wineries of Napa and Sonoma valleys offer more indulgent pleasures. East of the city, Berkeley is dominated by its university, which has given rise to a thriving bookstore and café scene, and sits just north of the gritty port city of Oakland.

North Beach

»» SAN FRANCISCO AT A GLANCE

◂ Russian Hill

Fisherman's Wharf

It may be a bit of an overrun tourist trap, but it does have a few points of irresistible tacky waterfront interest, and it's from here that you can catch a ferry to the prison of Alcatraz.

▸ Fisherman's Wharf

The "Hills"

What San Francisco is probably best known for – Nob, Telegraph and Russian hills form a tight, picturesque nucleus in the city's northeast corner.

North Beach

Next door to teeming Chinatown in the city center, this Italian-American enclave and old beatnik haunt is still replete with delis, restaurants, and cafés serving excellent espresso.

The Mission

Southwest of downtown and centered on Valencia Street, the heart of the city's Latino culture beats here.

The Castro

Just west of the Mission, this neighborhood has long been synonymous with gay activism and pride.

▸ The Castro

Golden Gate Park ▸

Chinatown

A tightly packed wedge of markets, shops and restaurants just a stone's throw from downtown's skyscrapers – but a world away, culturally.

Golden Gate Park

The expansive, man-made rectangle of greenery in the western sector is home to a brace of fine museums and several quiet gardens, each with its own theme.

SoMa

Once the area's central industrial zone, the region south of Market Street was also briefly the hub of the Internet boom of the 1990s; these days it's home to some fantastic institutions like the Museum of Modern Art and the much-loved SBC Park, where the baseball Giants play.

Hayes Valley

A quiet, little-known corner of the city located just east of Haight-Ashbury's tie-dyed emporiums, and a superb place to browse for fashion and funky homewares.

Chinatown ▸

Ideas

The big six sights

There are a handful of sights that define San Francisco, whether it's highbrow culture, brisk outdoorsiness, or Latin heritage. So however brief your visit may be, these half-dozen landmarks constitute must-see stops for anyone who hopes to understand the heart and soul of the city.

Golden Gate Bridge

As much an architectural as an engineering feat, built in 1937, this remains the most beautiful, and arguably the most photographed, bridge in the world.

▸P. 102 ▸ PACIFIC HEIGHTS & NORTHERN WATERFRONT

Mission Dolores

The oldest building in the city was thrown up by the first Spanish settlers; it's survived more than 200 years in remarkable condition.

▸P. 119 ▸ SOMA

SF Museum of Modern Art

This showstopping building by Swiss architect Mario Botta was an instant, crowd-pleasing hit as soon as it opened in 1995.

▸ P. 106 ▸ SOMA ▲

Union Square

Downtown's hub may be rimmed by alluring retail outlets, but a renovation has transformed it into a stand-alone attraction and a great place to relax with a coffee.

▸ P. 67 ▸ UNION SQUARE, THEATER DISTRICT & FINANCIAL DISTRICT ▲

Cable Cars

No-one should visit the city without taking a ride on these rickety but reliable trams, which vie with the Golden Gate Bridge as the city's most visible symbol.

▸ P. 69 ▸ UNION SQUARE, THEATER DISTRICT & FINANCIAL DISTRICT ▼

Alcatraz

This isolated prison was once home to America's nastiest criminals; today it's a moody and evocative place to linger for an afternoon.

▸ P. 95 ▸ FISHERMAN'S WHARF & ALCATRAZ ▼

Golden Gate park

The urban planners who masterminded San Francisco's rapid expansion in the last decades of the nineteenth century were forward-thinking enough to set aside a swathe of land in what was then the city's wild western edge to be a permanent park. That green space still stands today and is filled with a vast range of attractions and distractions.

Conservatory of Flowers

This recently overhauled, Victorian era hothouse is home to a stunning array of exotic and unusual plants.

▸ P. 138 ▸ GOLDEN GATE PARK ▾

Japanese Tea Garden

Come sit and sip amid the bonsai trees, statues and pagodas of a turn-of-the-century Japanese garden – in the heart of San Francisco.

▸ P. 137 ▸ GOLDEN GATE PARK ▾

AIDS Grove

A secluded, woodsy memorial garden that was the first of its kind in the country to commemorate victims of AIDS and HIV.

▸P. 139 ▸ GOLDEN GATE PARK ▲

Shakespeare Garden

Use the handy plaque here to count how many plants and flowers the Bard built into his works – and then try to find your favorite growing in the garden

▸P. 139 ▸ GOLDEN GATE PARK ▲

Buffalo Paddock

A park just isn't a park without its own herd of bison.

▸P. 139 ▸ GOLDEN GATE PARK ▼

Strybing Arboretum

Escape the more crowded sections of the park and stroll among the thousands of varieties of plants from all over the world on display here.

▸P. 139 ▸ GOLDEN GATE PARK ▼

Green San Francisco

One of the things that sets San Francisco so far apart from other American cities is its obsession with the **outdoors** – drive **minutes** across any bridge on the Bay, and within minutes you're in easy reach of beautiful, strenuous hiking and biking trails. But even within the city itself there are plenty of **green spaces** perfect for a walk, jog, or a relaxing time in the sun (or fog, as the case may be). Golden Gate Park is the first spot to make for; after that, check out any of the following.

Dolores Park

The Mission's main green space is perched on the side of a hill and offers rolling views across the city.

▸ P. 119 ▸ THE MISSION ▾

Land's End

Ramblers will enjoy this wilderness park that hugs the cliffs on the city's north-western tip and overlooks the Pacific Ocean.

▸ P. 142 ▸ THE RICHMOND & THE SUNSET ▾

Alamo Square

Though the views from the park, perched on a hill, are impressive enough, it's the overlooking row of fastidiously restored Victorian houses that draws shutterbugs.

▸ P. 132 ▸ HAIGHT-ASHBURY & AROUND ▲

The Presidio

For a break from the bustle of downtown, spend a day ambling round this former military base that's quilted with hiking trails and cycling paths.

▸ P. 101 ▸ PACIFIC HEIGHTS & THE NORTHERN WATERFRONT ▼

Washington Square Park

Come here early in the morning to see swathes of elderly local Chinese practicing t'ai chi together.

▸ P. 82 ▸ NORTH BEACH ▲

Chic hotels

Of course, if you want a reliable, if uninspiring, room run by one of the global chains, there are plenty of choices close to downtown. But San Francisco specializes in **boutique hotels** and **quirky guesthouses**: if you value a more individualistic experience and local feel, try one of the following, all of which are in or close to the city center. They include two converted schools (one for wayward boys, the other for convent girls), plus a landmark hotel given a witty, postmodern makeover by Philippe Starck.

Mosser

A hotel with three key advantages: a handy location close to Union Square, rock-bottom rates and a funky Modernist-meets-Victoriana vibe.

▸P. 168 ▸ ACCOMMODATION

Hotel Palomar

A chic, Art Nouveau-inspired bolthole on Market Street, its snug rooms fitted out in dark, smoky colors.

▸P. 169 ▸ ACCOMMODATION

Archbishop's Mansion

Every room at this luxurious B&B on Alamo Square – actually built in 1904 for the city's new archbishop – is named after an opera and decorated to match.

▸ P. 170 ▸ ACCOMMODATION ▲

Queen Anne Hotel

Once a girls' school, and possibly haunted, there's history to spare in this extravagantly decorated hotel in Pacific Heights.

▸ P. 168 ▸ ACCOMMODATION ▲

Clift Hotel

A Theater District hotel that provides plenty of ultracool jet-set minimalism, compliments of Philippe Starck; all for a steep price, but well worth it.

▸ P. 165 ▸ ACCOMMODATION ▼

Gay San Francisco

An estimated one in every five locals is either gay, lesbian, bisexual or transgender, so San Francisco more than earns its unofficial ranking as the most **gay-friendly** destination in the world. From dance clubs to sex clubs, from sites of protest to sights of progress, there's nowhere better to understand the history of gay liberation – or to get dressed up and strut down the street with pride.

The Stud

Bar-club that's a legendary, longtime local hangout, best on Tuesday's fabulous drag-inflected freakshow, "Trannyshack".

▸P. 112 ▸ SOMA

Dolores Beach

On a hot summer weekend, this patch of the Dolores Park is a splendid place to lay out and catch some sun – and a little attention.

▸P. 119 ▸ THE MISSION ▼

Folsom Street Fair

Known year-round for its profusion of leather bars, this street's annual fest encourages fetishists to let their freak flags fly.

▸P. 108 ▸ SOMA ▼

The Castro

This neighborhood is to San Francisco what the city is to the rest of the country: the epicenter of gay culture.

▸P. 126 ▸ THE CASTRO ▲

Armistead Maupin

The author of *Tales of the City* gave San Francisco's gay multitudes an iconic piece of literature to call their own.

▸P. 105 ▸ PACIFIC HEIGHTS AND THE NORTHERN WATERFRONT ▲

Local labels

This may be the city that turned the world blue and khaki one pair of pants at a time (thanks to the Gap and Levi's, which were both founded here), but there's much more to **shopping** in San Francisco than corporate megastores. We've scoured the streets for the best finds in local labels: pick up a pair of shoes or a pulp paperback at one of these stores, and you can be sure it's a unique souvenir.

Paolo Iantorno

A local shoemaking superstar, Iantorno designs and produces limited editions of men's and women's funky footwear which costs around $200 per pair.

▸P. 133 ▸ HAIGHT-ASHBURY & AROUND

Kayo

This bookstore's a pulp fiction paradise, with piles of vintage paperbacks both budget and premium priced.

▸P. 71 ▸ UNION SQUARE, THEATER DISTRICT & FINANCIAL DISTRICT

Amoeba Records

Vast, warehouse-like music store wedged into the western end of Haight-Ashbury – the best place to buy (or sell) music in the city.

P. 133 ▸ HAIGHT-ASHBURY & AROUND ▲

True Sake

A unique, sleek store that sells only Japanese rice wine – more than 100 varieties – and whose owner will happily spend time explaining the subtleties of sake.

P. 134 ▸ HAIGHT-ASHBURY & AROUND ▲

Velvet DaVinci

Gem-like jewelry store-cum-gallery, showcasing a wide range of local designers: pricey, but a dazzling place to browse.

P. 134 ▸ HAIGHT-ASHBURY & AROUND ▲

Oui, Three Queens

Whether it's for a wedding or a night out, the people at this shoebox-sized slice of salon surreality will ensure you look your best.

P. 133 ▸ HAIGHT-ASHBURY & AROUND ▲

Museums

The city may not be quite on a par with New York or LA in terms of overall fine arts holdings, but its **specialized collections** hold their own: bronze maquettes by Rodin, steel ropes running 24 hours a day, and wrought metal money trees, to name a few. Here are four of the best places to pick up a little cultural cachet, and if that's too intellectually taxing, one downtown museum devoted to nothing but cartoons.

Cartoon Art Museum

Cute but not cutesy, this museum offers exciting exhibitions that combine childhood favorites with more challenging, adult-aimed artwork.

▸P. 106 ▸ SOMA

Cable Car Museum

Come here to really see how those colorful, rickety cars manage to clamber so nimbly up the city's steep hills.

▸P. 89 ▸ NOB HILL, RUSSIAN HILL & TELEGRAPH HILL

Asian Art Museum

Crammed with antiquities from every country in Asia, this museum's also notable for the shimmering conversion of an old Beaux Arts building (not to mention its tasty café).

▸P. 115 ▸ THE TENDERLOIN & CIVIC CENTER ▼

California Palace of the Legion of Honor

The range and depth of the Rodin holdings here make this, hands down, the most impressive and important museum in town.

▸P. 141 ▸ THE RICHMOND & THE SUNSET ▲

Museum of Modern Art

Highlights of the museum's collection include pieces by the so-called California School (Frida Kahlo and Diego Rivera among others), as well as irreverent oddities from the likes of Jeff Koons.

▸P. 106 ▸ SOMA ▼

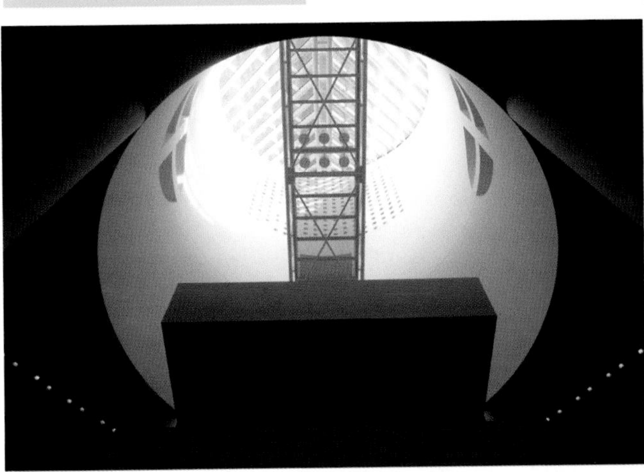

Spiritual San Francisco

The first **church** in town, the Mission Dolores, dates back to 1791, and has remained culturally important ever since – even if it does now share its status as Catholic stronghold with the much more modern St Mary's of the Assumption. In addition to these, a few other **places of worship** merit a visit on grounds of architectural interest or inviting atmosphere, no matter what your religious beliefs.

Mission Dolores

The simplicity of this centuries-old building makes it the most spiritual and welcoming of any church in the city.

▸P. 119 ▸ THE MISSION ▲

St Mary's Cathedral

Unfairly derided by many locals for its uncompromising modernist design, this sweeping, curving cathedral's an impressive sight inside and out.

▸P. 98 ▸ PACIFIC HEIGHTS & THE NORTHERN WATERFRONTR ▼

Grace Cathedral

A grand, Neo-Gothic church, gussied up with expensive touches like the reproduction Renaissance panels from Florence, Italy.

▸P. 89 ▸ NOB HILL, RUSSIAN HILL & TELEGRAPH HILL ▼

Waverley Place temples

It's worth detouring to see the temples hidden here in several old tenements for their combination of old world China and modern Chinatown.

▸P. 76 ▸ CHINATOWN & JACKSON SQUARE ▲

Church of St Peter & Paul

Look for the twin turrets that loom over North Beach and mark its spiritual center.

▸P. 82 ▸ NORTH BEACH ▲

Kids' San Francisco

There are few stresses when traveling with **kids** in San Francisco, other than the tiring hills: most **restaurants** will welcome young ones and there are **reduced rates** for almost every attraction or amenity. You can add to all that a handful of **sights** guaranteed to enchant any child.

Musée Méchanique

Dozens of arcade games jostle for attention in the buzzing, noisy museum overlooking the water – bring plenty of quarters if you want to enjoy them.

▸ P. 94 ▸ FISHERMAN'S WHARF & ALCATRAZ

Golden Gate Park

There's a carousel and a playground here, but this park's appeal for families comes just as much from its broad green lawns and peaceful calm.

▸ P. 137 ▸ GOLDEN GATE PARK

Ghirardelli Square

Touristy or not, this is the place where modern chocolate was invented, and it would be a crime not to sample one of the lush, sauce-doused sundaes at the gift shop's café.

▸P. 94 ▸ FISHERMAN'S WHARF & ALCATRAZ ▲

Exploratorium

The standout exhibit at this kid-centric science showcase is the sensory-depriving Tactile Dome, a pitch-black romp through touch, taste, smell and sound.

▸P. 101 ▸ PACIFIC HEIGHTS & THE NORTHERN WATERFRONT ▲

San Francisco Zoo

Make sure not to miss the zoo's two female Asian elephants, Calle and Tinkerbell, at their daily training sessions at 1.30pm.

▸P. 144 ▸ THE RICHMOND AND THE SUNSET ▼

San Francisco calendar

As with any major city, **celebrations** of all sorts happen year round, but things are taken to an extreme here. San Franciscans like dressing up, and they'll jump at any chance to put on a **costume** – the more outrageous the better. One byproduct of this tendency is that festivals are mostly riotous and all-inclusive affairs; just remember to bring a mask and some makeup if you want to join in.

Cherry Blossom Festival

Japantown's transformed into a riot of pale pink flowers during this springtime festival, which culminates in the selection of a Cherry Blossom Queen.

▸P. 180 ▸ ESSENTIALS

Halloween

Yet another opportunity for the city's eccentrics to slip into costume, this parade – which usually centers on the Castro – is a marathon of make-up, sequins and scary outfits.

▸P. 180 ▸ESSENTIALS

Chinese New Year

In late January or early February, both of the city's Chinatowns – downtown and the Richmond – pause for a day to celebrate the arrival of the New Year with a lively parade, street performers and stalls.

▸P. 179 ▸ ESSENTIALS ▲

Cinco de Mayo

Though only a regional fiesta back in Mexico that commemorates a nineteenth-century victory over the French, this holiday is celebrated by expat Latinos across America – and the Mission is one of the liveliest spots to enjoy it.

▸P. 180 ▸ ESSENTIALS ▶

Gay Pride

Late June each year is the time when San Francisco's LGBT community takes over the streets for a raucous and raunchy parade, though it's the quieter offshoot events in and around the Castro that are often far more fun.

▸P. 180 ▸ ESSENTIALS ◀

San Francisco specialties

The waves of immigrants who've settled in San Francisco have left their mark on the city – mostly in its menus: in a single day, you can nibble on Cantonese **dim sum**, recharge with **espresso** stiff enough for a Roman and gorge yourself on homemade **tacos**. Even better, you can try the city's **homegrown specialties** like steam beer, a byproduct of warm days and thirsty early locals, who couldn't afford the ice to brew bitter so fermented their yeast at room temperature and created a brand new beer.

Steam beer

Don't worry about the watery name – the locally produced brews, known as "steam beers," have the hearty taste of bitter but the lower alcohol content of lager; you can sample it at microbreweries like the Thirsty Bear.

▸P. 110 ▸ SOMA

Dim sum

These snack-sized portions are served from trolleys in restaurants across town,; ask about any off-menu, insiders' specials.

▸P. 79 ▸ CHINATOWN & JACKSON SQUARE ▲

Tacos

You can't leave town without sampling one of these sloppy, cheap, and delicious treats, San Francisco's unofficial snack of choice.

▸P. 122 ▸ THE MISSION ▲

Boudin sourdough bread

For reasons so far unexplained, the yeast that sours this dough can't survive outside the city, so try it while you can.

▸P. 96 ▸ FISHERMAN'S WHARF & ALCATRAZ ▼

Espresso in an Italian caffè

Only cowards order cappuccino.

▸P. 83 ▸ NORTH BEACH ▼

Bars

If you want a quiet cocktail accompanied by a soft jazz soundtrack, San Francisco can serve both the music and the martini; while if you're more the Red Bull and remix type, there's a couple of brand new bars with both drinks and dancefloors. For everything in between – grungy pubs in the Mission, beatnik hangouts in North Beach – the vast range of **drinking spots** on offer should more than fill your needs.

Bambuddha

New Age-inspired bar-cum-lounge with feng shui-respecting fountains and a smooth, Ibizan house soundtrack.

▸P. 117 ▸ THE TENDERLOIN & CIVIC CENTER

Li Po's

Raucous, kitschy bar popular with Chinatown locals and used by Wayne Wang as a setting for his movie *Chan is Missing*.

▸P. 80 ▸ CHINATOWN & JACKSON SQUARE

Harry Denton's Starlight Room

A sophisticated downtown hotel bar, known for its killer martinis and the jazzy soundtrack provided by the Starlight Orchestra every evening.

▸P. 74 ▸ UNION SQUARE, THEATER DISTRICT & FINANCIAL DISTRICT ▼

Edinburgh Castle

Eccentric, Scottish-themed bar, filled with Highland memorabilia but actually run by Koreans – it's renowned for the superb facsimile of fish'n'chips it offers as part of the pub food menu.

▸P. 118 ▸ THE TENDERLOIN & CIVIC CENTER ▲

The Redwood Room

The postmodern renovation of this landmark bar retained the rich redwood paneling, but added quirky touches like shimmering, ever-shifting electronic portraits on the walls.

▸P. 74 ▸ UNION SQUARE, THEATER DISTRICT & FINANCIAL DISTRICT ▶

Cultural San Francisco

Of all things – and there are many – that San Franciscans have to brag about, they are most proud of their city's performing arts. With a world-class symphony orchestra and ballet, not to mention a raft of reliably high-quality fringe venues, this is a city that takes the arts very seriously . . . and yet still finds room for more campy, outré entertainment.

San Francisco Symphony

The antics of conductor Michael Tilson Thomas may divide critics, but it's undeniable that he's reinvigorated the local orchestra with a program heavy on twentieth-century composers.

▸P. 118 ▸ THE TENDERLOIN & CIVIC CENTER ▲

Yerba Buena Center for the Arts

This new downtown venue is the best place in the city to catch avant-garde dance and theatre.

▸P. 112 ▸ SOMA ▾

The Roxie movie theater

From obscure documentaries about dog shelters to indie festival favorites, the Roxie shows them all thanks to its determinedly anti-mainstream programming.

▸P. 125 ▸ THE MISSION ▴

Theater Artaud

Converted warehouse in a quiet corner of the Mission that consistently turns out inventive, intriguing and, best of all, accessible dance shows and dramas.

▸P. 125 ▸ THE MISSION ▾

City Lights Bookstore

Lawrence Ferlinghetti, poet and owner of this literary landmark, was a early champion of the Beats (Jack Kerouac and Allen Ginsberg among others).

▸P. 81 ▸ NORTH BEACH ▴

Funky food

San Francisco proudly (and somewhat unverifiably) claims to be second only to Paris in the number of restaurants within its city limits; and there's a bewildering selection of cuisines, prices, and atmospheres on offer. To help you navigate, we've singled out five **funky favorites** that are always a great place to grab a well-priced meal.

Luna Park

A groovy restaurant that attracts a diverse crowd, from young hipsters to older intellectual types, all of whom come for the simple, delicious modern American food.

▸P. 124 ▸ THE MISSION

Mecca

Part swanky supper club, part slick fusion eatery, this Castro mainstay is a killer place for cocktails or dinner.

▸P. 129 ▸ THE CASTRO

Foreign Cinema

The gimmick here is that diners can enjoy a classic movie while they eat, but the real reason to come is the tasty, well-prepared French food.

▸P. 123 ▸ THE MISSION ▲

Home

The name says it all: Home serves up cozy comfort food to a largely local crowd of regulars. The patio's a prime place to grab a drink on summer weekends.

▸P. 129 ▸ THE CASTRO ▲

EOS

Modern restaurant just off Haight-Ashbury's main drag that specializes in East-West fusion food – the prices may be high, but it's an insiders' favorite.

▸P. 135 ▸ HAIGHT-ASHBURY & AROUND ▼

Cafés

You can still sample some of San Francisco's fabled food even if your budget's more fish and chips than foie gras. Many of the city's cafés can hold their own against more upscale eateries, especially if you want to try **exotic** or **ethnic** cuisines in a more relaxed environment where you can feel comfortable lingering. While you slurp that oyster or sip your coffee, you may well be sitting next to one of the city's top chefs, who are partial to the rockbottom prices and sky-high quality of many of the places listed here.

Caffe Trieste

An old school Italian staple in the heart of North Beach, where Francis Ford Coppola is said to have knocked out the first draft of the script for *The Godfather*.

P. 83 ▸ NORTH BEACH

Swan Oyster Depot

Grab a stool at this cramped but fun seafood café and wolf down the cheap but delicious oysters on offer.

P. 117 ▸ THE TENDERLOIN & CIVIC CENTER

Saigon Sandwiches

A hole-in-the-wall sandwich shop that serves cheap, pork-crammed sandwiches slathered with delicious, sinus-clearing chile sauce.

▸P. 117 ▸ THE TENDERLOIN & CIVIC CENTER ▲

Café Flore

Cruisey but fun Castro corner café, with an outdoor patio that's ideal for a long, leisurely Sunday afternoon reading the papers and checking out passers-by.

▸P. 128 ▸ THE CASTRO ▼

Late-night San Francisco

If there's one complaint justifiably leveled at San Francisco, it's how early everything closes here; after all, most locals want to be up, out and exercising long before 7am (if they're not already expected in the office by then). For resolute **night owls**, though, we've picked out the places that are live and kicking well into the early hours – even, in some cases, until those crack-of-dawn joggers start filling the streets.

Bagdad Café

This diner's definitely a no-frills, no-fuss option but it's one of the few places in town open 24 hours.

▸ P. 128 ▸ THE CASTRO

The Globe

Late-night eating doesn't preclude the possibility of fine dining; here you can; expect to share drinks or dinner with the dozens of waitstaff from other restaurants who flock here once their shifts end.

▸ P. 79 ▸ CHINATOWN & JACKSON SQUARE

El Farolito taqueria

The best time to come to this age-old Mission taqueria is late at night, when club kids and late-shift workers sit alongside one another at its refectory tables.

▸P. 122 ▸ THE MISSION 

Castro Street

The raucous nightlife here revs up a gear as places elsewhere start closing – and as an added bonus, each bar's no more than a minute's stumble from the next.

▸P. 130 ▸ THE CASTRO ▼

Chinatown Nightmarket

Portsmouth Square is a riot of squawking music and crowded stalls when this market's in session, selling everything from clothes to toys and souvenirs.

▸P. 77 ▸ CHINATOWN & JACKSON SQUARE ▲

San Francisco for free

Splurged on a five-star meal, and need to save some cash? Want to take home a pricey case of Sonoma chardonnay and have to economize in the meantime? Never fear. There are plenty of ways to see and enjoy the city without once opening your wallet – none of the activities listed here will cost you a penny.

Meditate at the Palace of Fine Arts

It's the stillness and simplicity of the grounds, especially the reflecting pool, which give this doleful holdover from a grand exhibition such power.

P. 101 ▸ PACIFIC HEIGHTS & THE NORTHERN WATERFRONT

Walk across Golden Gate Bridge

It's only when you cross it on foot that you can really enjoy the views of the city as well as understanding the sheer, breath-taking scale of the bridge.

P. 102 ▸ PACIFIC HEIGHTS & THE NORTHERN WATERFRONT

SF MOMA first Tuesday of the month

This is an unmissable local standout – and it's even better to stop by when it's free for everyone.

P. 106 ▸ SOMA ▲

Baker Beach

Catch some sun on the city's best and cleanest beach, nestled on the peninsula's northwestern rim.

P. 143 ▸ THE RICHMOND & THE SUNSET ▲

Take a City Guides walking tour

Free city tours, run by enthusiastic and chatty amateur historians, on a wide range of topics.

P. 178 ▸ ESSENTIALS ▼

Sunday gospel services at Glide Memorial Church

Catch one of the goosebump-inducing gospel services at this charitable church, but make sure to arrive at least two hours in advance for a prime seat.

P. 113 ▸ THE TENDERLOIN & CIVIC CENTER ▼

Gourmet San Francisco

It's hard to pinpoint exactly why and how San Francisco's obsession with **food** began, but many historians point to the Gold Rush. That's when thousands of men swamped the city, took up rooms in boarding houses and demanded a daily meal from the local restaurant. Hordes of eateries appeared in response, and today eating out is still one of the city's number one obsessions.

Molinari's

Old-school deli on the main drag in North Beach, staffed by Italians and decked out with swinging salamis and a smelly, delicious cheese counter.

▸P. 83 ▸ NORTH BEACH ▲

Ferry Plaza Farmers Market

This is a swish showcase for local produce, whether meats, fruits or vegetables, with a handy selection of equally gourmet restaurants and bars on site too.

▸P. 71 ▸ UNION SQUARE, THEATER DISTRICT & FINANCIAL DISTRICT ▲

Jardinière

Chef Traci des Jardins is a local culinary rockstar, and this is her flagship, namesake restaurant: try the six-course tasting menu to see what the fuss is about.

▸P. 117 ▸ THE TENDERLOIN & CIVIC CENTER ▼

Gary Danko

Chef Danko's namesake eatery is widely acknowledged as the top restaurant in town. Wallet-busting but worth it.

▸P. 97 ▸ FISHERMAN'S WHARF & ALCATRAZ ▼

Greens

Vegetarian cuisine's big gourmet business in the city, and the poshest place for a plate of portobello mushrooms is Greens, where you can also enjoy the views across the bay to Marin.

▸P. 104 ▸ FISHERMAN'S WHARF & ALCATRAZ ▲

Chez Panisse

Alice Waters, the chef-owner here, is the woman credited with inventing California cuisine, the light, ingredient-driven style of cooking that started in San Francisco and soon spread across the world.

▸P. 152 ▸ BERKELEY ▲

Sports and outdoors

Sneakers are the smartest choice of footwear in San Francisco – with so many steep hills to navigate, stilettos are hardly a practical option. But there's another reason everyone should pack a pair of Pumas: the **sporting scene**. This is an athlete's city, whether you want to catch a game of **baseball**, **skate** around a park, or **pedal** across the Golden Gate bridge; afterwards, you can soothe those aching muscles at a Japanese steam room

Giants' baseball

The San Francisco Giants' SBC Park, set right by the water, was built to maximize the home run totals of the great Barry Bonds

▸P. 108 ▸ SOMA

Biking around the Presidio

There's no wilder green space in easy reach of downtown, and the vast park here's a struggle to cover on foot; better to rent a bike and cycle its network of looping paths.

▸P. 101 ▸ PACIFIC HEIGHTS & THE NORTHERN WATERFRONT

Rollerblading in Golden Gate Park

Join the hordes of locals who on weekends strap on their blades and slice through the park, from the eastern edge at the Panhandle all the way west to Ocean Beach.

▸P. 137 ▸ GOLDEN GATE PARK ▼

Kabuki Hot Springs

A trendy, converted Japanese bathhouse in the JapanCenter that's a relaxing place to lounge or grab a massage, even for determined spa-phobes.

▸P. 99 ▸ PACIFIC HEIGHTS & THE NORTHERN WATERFRONT ▲

Out of the city

It's easy to take a day-trip out of the city: rent a bike to get across the Golden Gate Bridge, and you'll be in the wilds of the **Marin Headlands**, convenient for the charming port of **Sausalito**. **Berkeley** or **Oakland** are easier options – just 15 minutes' ride by BART– and offer up a nice contrast to each other (and to San Francisco itself): the former quite artsy and freewheeling, the latter a no-nonsense, working-class town.

Bookstores on Telegraph Ave

It's not surprising that a town as student-oriented as Berkeley would have so many bookstores – though it is a pleasant shock that the stock's so wide-ranging and literate.

▸ P. 150 ▸ BERKELEY

Oakland Museum

The three-tier exhibition here is a fun and exhaustive look at California's history, ecology and art.

▸ P. 155 ▸ OAKLAND

Sausalito

This gritty old fishing port has been prettified into a charming, if self-consciously quaint, seaside resort.

▸ P. 159 ▸ EXCURSIONS ▲

Heinold's First and Last Chance Saloon

A rickety old saloon that's a must-see pilgrimage site for Jack London fans – the writer was a regular.

▸ P. 155 ▸ OAKLAND ▼

UCAL-Berkeley campus

The university's surprisingly woodsy and bucolic campus is full of nooks and lawns where anyone's welcome to lounge.

▸ P. 147 ▸ BERKELEY ▼

The music scene

Jam bands? A San Francisco invention, thanks to the Grateful Dead. Acid Jazz? The first bands bubbled up in the Bay Area. Post-grunge punk pop? Seattle could only watch Green Day in envy. Little wonder then that the San Francisco music scene today – both live performers and the innovative DJ community – is as vibrant as ever: the **venues** below are the best places to take its pulse.

Bimbo's 365 Club

Don't be put off by the name – this is one of the most reliable venues for gigs by interesting, big name acts and a few off-beat tribute bands.

▸ P. 86 ▸ NORTH BEACH

Fillmore Auditorium

Once the hub of San Francisco's counterculture scene, this large space reopened ten years ago and now hosts regular rock and alt-rock concerts.

▸P. 105 ▸ PACIFIC HEIGHTS & THE NORTHERN WATERFRONT ◂

Boom Boom Room

Once owned by the late John Lee Hooker, the stage here usually offers fine touring blues and funk performers.

▸P. 105 ▸ PACIFIC HEIGHTS & THE NORTHERN WATERFRONT ▸

DNA Lounge

A hi-tech combination dance club and performance space – you can check out the scene in advance thanks to its regular webcasts.

▸P. 112 ▸ SOMA ◂

Sublounge

Serving a refreshingly mature and musically astute crowd, this Mission lounge specializes in progressive house (with an occasional evening devoted to old school funk).

▸P. 125 ▸ THE MISSION ▸

San Francisco inventions

The pioneering spirit of San Francisco not only fueled the Gold Rush, but made the city home to some major cultural firsts – whether transforming denim from an also-ran fabric from France into a workwear wonder, making going topless a reason for tipping or even combining cookies and kooky predictions.

Chop Suey

Its exact origins are murky, but many claim that this dish – whose name derives from the Chinese character meaning "odds and ends" – was invented by Chinese-American laborers in San Francisco in the late nineteenth century.

▸ P. 79 ▸ CHINATOWN & JACKSON SQUARE

Blue jeans

Levi Strauss came to the city planning to supply tents and wagon covers to Gold Rush miners, but ended up turning his tough fabric into work pants.

▸ P. 88 ▸ NOB HILL, RUSSIAN HILL & TELEGRAPH HILL

Fortune Cookie

Though Chinese-Americans in Los Angeles filed a rival claim to cooking up the idea, most people acknowledge Japanese Makota Hagiwara, who worked in the Japanese Tea Garden, as having created these as a token of thanks in 1907.

▸ P. 137 ▸ GOLDEN GATE PARK ▲

Cocoa butter

Gold miner-turned-grocer Domenico Ghirardelli discovered how to sweat the tasty butter out of raw cocoa – and made millions without panning a single nugget.

▸ P. 94 ▸ FISHERMAN'S WHARF & ALCATRAZ ▲

The Martini

A triumphant Gold Rush miner is said to have asked for champagne and instead been served the bartender's "special" – a cocktail made from gin and vermouth he said was named after the town of Martinez.

▸ P. 74 ▸ UNION SQUARE, THEATER DISTRICT & FINANCIAL DISTRICT ▼

Topless waitressing

At North Beach's Condor Club, waitress Carol "44 inches" Doda rolled down her top one day in 1964, and so ensured herself bigger tips and a place in history.

▸ P. 82 ▸ NORTH BEACH ▼

Murals

Public art, often powered by protest, has long been welcomed in San Francisco; undoubtedly the local mural mastermind was Mexican transplant Diego Rivera. His thumpingly socialist artwork was the cause of much controversy back in the 1930s; today, it's revered rather than reviled, as evidenced by the many other modern murals that echo Rivera's style and concerns.

Diego Rivera murals, Coit Tower

The muscular murals around the base of this landmark are as artistically impressive today as they were when first painted in the 1930s, even if their communist sympathies are far less controversial.

▸P. 87 ▸NOB HILL, RUSSIAN HILL & TELEGRAPH HILL ▲

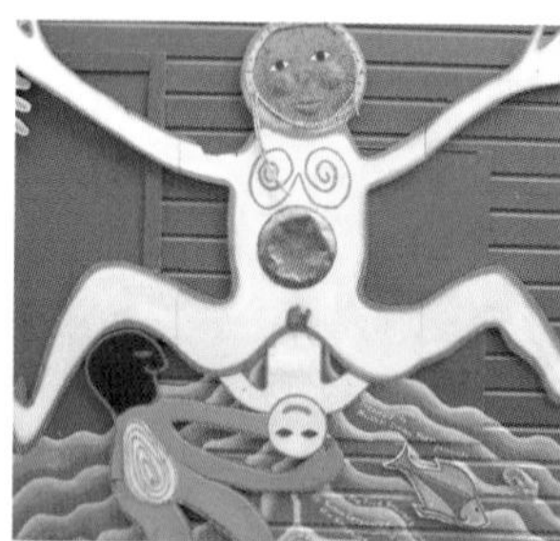

Balmy Alley

This tiny alleyway's an ever-shifting gallery of protest art, as small murals are painted on wooden fences and replaced as soon as the colors fade.

▸P. 121 ▸ THE MISSION ▲

Women's Building

Seven female designers plotted this massive mural, which tattoos the exterior of a community center, though it's more politically than artistically notable.

▸P. 121 ▸ THE MISSION

Diego Rivera mural, SF Art Institute

A massive mural that exemplifies Rivera's art – from the socialist, worker-friendly theme to the contrariness of placing himself in the picture, albeit with his back to the viewer.

▸P. 89 ▸ NOB HILL, RUSSIAN HILL & TELEGRAPH HILL

Maxfield Parrish mural, Palace Hotel

Parrish's sprightly picture, painted specially for the hotel, shows a troupe of children entranced by the Pied Piper of Hamelin.

▸P. 106 ▸ SOMA

Defenestration outdoor wall sculpture

Local artist Brian Goggin created this piece of public art by bolting furniture to the exterior of an abandoned building.

▸P. 108 ▸ SOMA

Only in San Francisco

Outsiders, non-conformists and even the downright crazy have always found a welcome in San Francisco – famously nonjudgmental, this is a place where eccentrics have commandeered the mainstream. In the past, drag queens dressed as nuns have stood for city council and commune-dwelling hippies have staged free food giveaways to counteract the evils of capitalism; today, that same spirit still thrives in the city – here's the best of the wacky, weird and wonderful.

JapanCenter Peace Pagoda

A modernist monument to the evils of the atomic age, this poured concrete pagoda resembles a pile of space-age mushrooms.

▸P. 99 ▸ PACIFIC HEIGHTS & THE NORTHERN WATERFRONT ▾

Tattoo Museum

If you're too squeamish to go under the needle yourself, you can always browse the selection of vintage tools and designs on display here.

▸P. 82 ▸ NORTH BEACH ▾

Amateur Opera Hour

The best time to come to Caffe Trieste is on Saturday afternoons during amateur opera hour, when karaoke sopranos fill the café with an irresistible (if offkey) choice of arias.

▸P. 83 ▸ NORTH BEACH ▲

Clarion Music Center

The place to buy obscure instruments from around the world, as well as to catch an avant-garde performance of world music by little-known traveling musicians.

▸P. 80 ▸ CHINATOWN & JACKSON SQUARE ▲

Bay to Breakers Race

The ultimate fancy dress party, in the guise of a race across town: look for the wags dressed as salmon who run backwards – or rather, "swim upstream."

▸P. 180 ▸ ESSENTIALS ▼

Good Vibrations

Funky, friendly, and full of goodies, this store, run by a local collective, is a sex shop without shame.

▸P. 121 ▸ THE MISSION ▼

Views of San Francisco

Official statistics put the number of hills within the city limits at a calf-aching 43, but the three closest to downtown – Telegraph, Nob and Russian – are the ones every visitor is likely to encounter and scale. Sadly, the views from these vantage points are often obscured by buildings, so we've picked out five fine alternatives if you want to snag a **bird's-eye view** of the city.

Carnelian Room, Bank of America building

A rooftop cocktail lounge with gasp-inducing views across North Beach to Alcatraz – they're even better in the warm glow of dusk.

▶P. 73 ▶ UNION SQUARE, THEATER DISTRICT & FINANCIAL DISTRICT ▼

Coit Tower

Perched on top of Telegraph Hill, this concrete tower looks back over the Financial District's forest of skyscrapers, as well as across the bay to Berkeley.

▸P. 87 ▸ NOB HILL, RUSSIAN HILL & TELEGRAPH HILL ▲

Marin Headlands

Cycle, walk or drive across the Golden Gate Bridge to reach Marin, then swivel round to catch one of the best glimpses of the city's skyline.

▸P. 157 ▸ EXCURSIONS ▲

Campanile

On a cloudless day, you can see, beyond Berkeley's downtown, San Francisco bobbing on the horizon, its signature skyscrapers easily picked out against the sky.

▸P. 149 ▸ BERKELEY ▼

Alcatraz

Once you've finished exploring the deserted cells on "The Rock", walk down to the path which overlooks the city – on a clear day, there's a pristine view of downtown.

▸P. 95 ▸ FISHERMAN'S WHARF & ALCATRAZ ▼

San Francisco people

Though their names may not all be familiar, each of the adoptive or locally born San Franciscans we've cited here was a headline-grabber in their day, and left a lasting impact on the city; some through cash and connections, like the outrageous Alma de Bretteville, others in tougher times, like Harvey Milk, or through artistic endeavors, like Jack Kerouac.

Alma de Bretteville

Wild child Alma posed for the semi-nude statue in Union Square and then promptly snagged a rich husband, became Rodin's first major American patron, and finally endowed a majestic museum for that sculpture collection on her death.

▸P. 67 ▸ UNION SQUARE, THEATER DISTRICT & FINANCIAL DISTRICT ▼

Jack Kerouac

The handsome, swaggering Kerouac became an icon of the beat movement with the publication of his novel *On The Road*; the time he spent in San Francisco is commemorated with a street name.

▸P. 81 ▸ NORTH BEACH ▼

Dashiel Hammett

Several of Hammett's stories are set in the Westin St Francis Hotel – little wonder, as when working as a private detective in the 1920s, he was part of the team who investigated the rape and murder case against Fatty Arbuckle in the hotel.

▸P. 167 ▸ UNION SQUARE, THEATER DISTRICT & FINANCIAL DISTRICT ▲

Jack London

The self-taught writer was born in Oakland and seemed destined to be an orphaned delinquent until his talent prevailed. He's beloved enough to snag an entire waterfront complex named in his honor.

▸P. 153 ▸ OAKLAND ▲

Ambrose Bierce

Known for its secretive camping retreats by corporate honchos, the Bohemian Club was originally an arty breakfast club that counted writers like Bierce among its number.

▸P. 69 ▸ UNION SQUARE, THEATER DISTRICT & FINANCIAL DISTRICT ▼

Harvey Milk

The first openly gay local politician passed permanently into the history books when, along with mayor George Moscone, he was assassinated in City Hall by a disgruntled ex-colleague.

▸P. 113 ▸ THE TENDERLOIN & CIVIC CENTER ▼

Brunch

Don't wait till dinner to sample San Francisco's fabled food – **breakfast** and **brunch** is a prolonged gourmet affair here too. There are a few simple rules: bring a book (lines are always long and reservations rarely accepted), smile at the server (they're always harried), and always order the house special (it's guaranteed to be delicious).

Sears Fine Food

A downtown diner, with frilly tablecloths and friendly service, that makes a welcome change from the tourist traps nearby.

▸P. 72 ▸ UNION SQUARE, THEATER DISTRICT & FINANCIAL DISTRICT

Ti Couz

This leisurely crêperie offers traditional buckwheat Breton pancakes with savory fillings as well as lighter, sweet versions like crêpes suzette with orange liqueur.

▸P. 124 ▸THE MISSION

Café de la Presse

It may be overpriced, but this Francophile café's an irresistible lure on a Sunday morning for a foreign paper and huge, comforting café au lait.

▸ P. 78 ▸ CHINATOWN & JACKSON SQUARE ▾

Mama's

On weekends, the wait can be knee-achingly long, but it's certain to be worth it: there isn't a misstep on the marvelous menu.

▸ P. 83 ▸ NORTH BEACH ▴

Boogaloo's

This brightly colored diner serves Latin-inflected American brunch staples and showcases a rotating gallery of art on sale to raise money for disabled adults.

▸ P. 122 ▸ THE MISSION ▾

Places

Places

Union Square, Theater District, and Financial District

Three distinct neighborhoods form the core of San Francisco's downtown. Each is stitched along the northern edge of Market Street, which runs through the oldest parts of the city and binds the warehouse districts to the south with the chic shops and sleek offices immediately north. The most visited of these three neighborhoods is the shopping mecca of Union Square, which is fringed with upscale designer and department stores, not to mention hordes of hotels to house credit card-happy tourists. Immediately west stands the quieter and less commercial Theater District, its streets packed with old theaters, more hotels, and private clubs. Meanwhile, the land wedged between the San Francisco Bay and the eastern edge of Union Square is the canyon of skyscrapers known as the Financial District. It's mostly deserted at nights and on weekends but is home to San Francisco's signature building, the Transamerica Pyramid.

Union Square

Named after the Unionists who gathered to rally here on the eve of the Civil War, this square festered in recent years as a camping ground for the local hordes of the homeless but is now sparkling after a 2003 facelift. Now, the center's stepped and paved, dotted with potted plants like a cozy patio, its edges marked with stout, pineapple-like palm trees. There's a handy café (*Mocca*) on the eastern edge, and ample seating – ideal for a break after browsing the dozens of shops that rim the square. This neighborhood's known for its shopping, especially the massive *Macy's* megastore that fills the entire block south of the square.

There are two local landmarks on the square itself: the Corinthian column at its center commemorates a victory in the Spanish-American War but is more notable for the woman, Alma de Bretteville, who

▼ UNION SQUARE

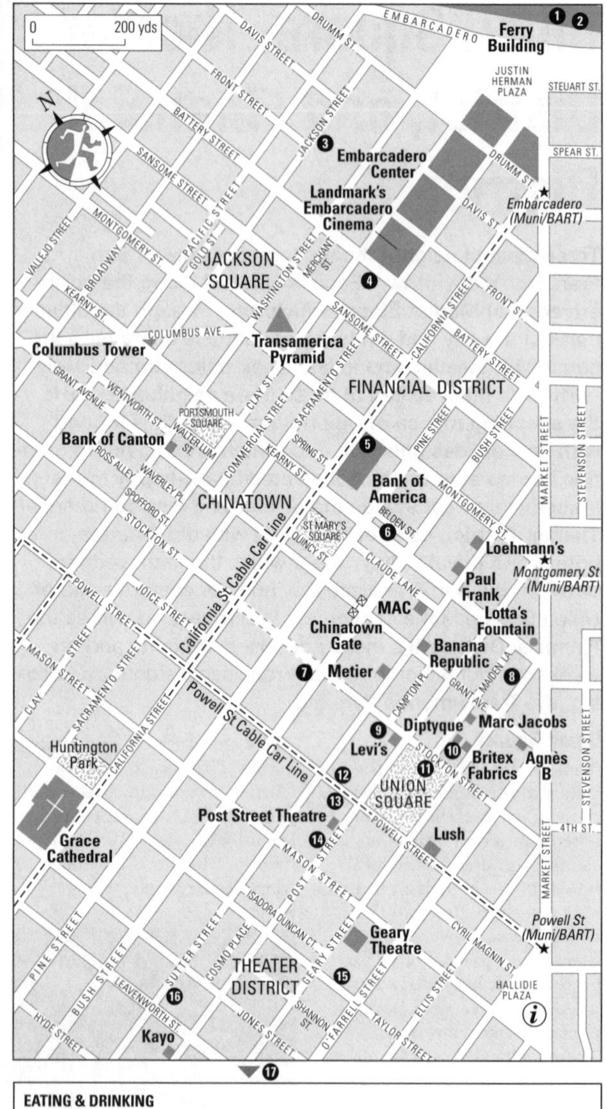

EATING & DRINKING

Asia de Cuba & Redwood Room	15	Grandviews Lounge	9	Red Room	16
Carnelian Room	5	Harry Denton's Starlight Room	12	Sears Fine Food	13
Emporio Rulli	11	Kokkari Estiatorio	3	Slanted Door	1
Farallon	14	Millennium	17	Tunnel Top	7
Ferry Plaza Wine Merchant	2	Mocca	10	Yank Sing	4
Ginger's Trois	6	Morrow's Nut House	8		

▲ MAIDEN LANE

scandalously posed for the scantily clad statue on its summit. De Bretteville was a wayward beauty who married sugar magnate Adolph Spreckels and then used his money to found the fantastic Legion of Honor art museum (see p.141) in the Richmond. The other landmark is the opulent *Westin St Francis Hotel* (see p.167) on the square's western edge.

Maiden Lane

Dedicated designer label lovers should head to the north end of Union Square where they'll find Maiden Lane, a small alleyway that was once a haven for hookers (hence the name) but is now known for its chic boutiques and upscale outdoor cafés.

Hallidie Plaza

Hallidie Plaza, at Powell and Market streets, is the one place in San Francisco through which just about every tourist will pass. The main San Francisco Visitors Information Center is here (see Essentials, p.175), overlooking a major Muni/BART train station; the plaza is also the terminus for the two cable car lines that run to the northern waterfront. The cable car was invented in 1873 by the plaza's namesake, Andrew Hallidie, an enterprising engineer who saw that San Francisco's hilly terrain would be better served by a mechanical alternative to horse-drawn carriages.

The Theater District

This neighborhood, sandwiched between gleaming Union Square and the grubby Tenderloin, is filled with hotels and old theaters. One of the most prominent theaters here is the *Geary*, a magnificent 1910 Beaux Arts building that was severely damaged in the 1989 earthquake, then reopened six years later after a massive retrofit, and now home to the American Conservatory Theater. The other impressive facade belongs to the *Alcazar Theatre* (650 Geary St at Leavenworth), which is a former Masonic Temple originally designed to resemble an Islamic mosque. Showy as these theaters are, the blocks of Post and Sutter streets that cut through this area are home to some of downtown's least visible landmarks: about fourteen private clubs, who draw their members from San Francisco's society elite and whose existence is evidenced only by discreet and sometimes enigmatic metal plaques (*The Bohemian Club*'s sign bears the motto: "Weaving Spider Come Not Here").

▼ HALLIDIE PLAZA

Bank of America Building

555 California St at Kearney ⓦwww.bankofamerica.com. The headquarters of California's largest financial institution, this enormous building was quite unpopular when finished in 1971; that's because its dark red granite facade offended architectural tastemakers, who wanted to preserve San Francisco's reputation as "a city of white." Affection's grown over the years for the broad-shouldered hulk, no doubt in part thanks to the stunning views from the *Carnelian Room* bar on its top floor (see p.58).

The Transamerica Pyramid

600 Montgomery St at Clay ⓣ415/983-4100, ⓦwww.tapyramid.com. One of the city's signature sights, the Transamerica Pyramid is a glossy Financial District landmark designed by LA-based architect William Pereira in 1972. Nicknamed "Pereira's Prick," thanks to its tapering, priapic shape, this once controversial structure looks more like a squared-off rocket than a pyramid. The building's filled with nondescript offices and sadly, there's no longer public access to the viewing platform on the 27th floor. This skyscraper also occupies the site of the celebrated **Montgomery Block**, a four-story building that was home away from home for the city's literati, including Robert Louis Stevenson and Mark Twain, in the nineteenth century. It was unfortunately torn down to make way for a parking lot in 1959, though there's a commemorative brass plaque in the lobby.

The Embarcadero

Thanks to the traffic-clogged double decker freeway that used to loom over the waterfront (torn down in 1992 after being fatally damaged by the 1989 earthquake), the Embarcadero was for years a no-go area. But once the freeway was gone, the area became a magnet for hotels and restaurants taking advantage of the magnificent views across the bay. Today, the area just inland from the waterfront is dominated by **The Embarcadero Center** (ⓦwww.embarcaderocenter.com): four massive skyscrapers and the mall that sprawls around their base, filled with shops and restaurants. At the east end of the mall sits the ugly modernist spectacle of **Vaillancourt Fountain**, which, on the last Friday of each month, is the meeting place for Critical Mass, when cyclists gather to promote bicycling as an environmentally friendly alternative to driving.

▼ VAILLANCOURT FOUNTAIN

The Ferry Building

at the foot of Market Street ⓣ415/693-0996, ⓦwww.ferrybuildingmarketplace.com. Sat 8:30am–1:30pm. Once the transit hub linking San Francisco with the East Bay, the Ferry Building, at the foot of Market Street, was renovated during the 1990s into a foodie mall, with artisanal cheese and chocolate shops, old-fashioned butchers, and local wine merchants, plus several noteworthy restaurants. To complement this conversion, the much-loved local **farmers market**, where produce growers hawk their wares and rock-star restaurateurs like Alice Waters can often be spotted browsing, has now moved into the main building and is a great place to grab a cheap gourmet lunch.

Shops

Agnès b

33 Grant Ave at Market ⓣ415/772-9995. Chic and very French, offering slinky, slimfit clothing for men and women.

▲ MACY'S

Banana Republic

256 Grant Ave at Sutter ⓣ415/788-3087. The vast flagship branch of this national chain is especially noteworthy for its location, The White House, a historic five-story mansion whose interior has simply been whitewashed and preserved to form an impressive, cavernous backdrop to the casual clothes on sale.

Britex Fabrics

146 Geary St at Stockton ⓣ415/392-2910. A local institution, selling fabric and trims, as well as more than 30,000 kinds of buttons.

Diptyque

171 Maiden Lane ⓣ415/402-0600, ⓦwww.diptyqueusa.com. One of only two boutiques outside France from this deluxe candlemaker – their Tuberose (rose) fragrance is a top seller.

Kayo

814 Post St at Leavenworth ⓣ415/749-0554. Wed–Sun 11am–6pm. Glorious vintage paperback bookstore, crammed with bargain classics that include pulpy mysteries, sci-fi, and campy 1950s sleaze fiction.

Levi's

300 Post St at Stockton ⓣ415/501-0100. Four levels of jeans, tops, and jackets set against a thumping backdrop of club music. This flagship store stocks the entire Levi's line; it also offers the "Original Spin" service, where you can order customized denim.

Loehmann's

222 Sutter St at Kearny ⓣ415/982-3215. Root around for terrific designer bargains at this upscale discounter that's often crammed with same-season finds from the likes of DKNY and BCBG.

Lush

240 Powell St at Geary ⓣ415/693-9633, ⓦwww.lush.co.uk. First US outpost for this British handmade cosmetics chain, known for its bubbling bath "bombs" that fizz around the tub while fragrancing the water.

MAC (Modern Appeal Clothing)

5 Claude Lane ⓣ415/837-1604. Men's branch of the hip and directional local boutique (not to be confused with the makeup line), stocking European designers like Wim Neels as well as exclusive suit designs from Armand Basi.

Marc Jacobs

125 Maiden Lane ⓣ415/362-6500. The patron saint of boho chic, Jacobs offers Forties-inspired shoes and colorful, thrift-store-like threads, albeit at designer prices.

Metier

355 Sutter St at Grant Ave ⓣ415/989-5395. A gallery of girly, up-and-coming clothing designers, like Mayle and Language. There's also high-end hipster wear from Development and antique-inspired jewelry by Cathy Waterman.

Paul Frank

262 Sutter St at Kearny ⓣ415/374-2758, ⓦwww.paulfrank.com. Plenty of cutesy, cartoony accessories here, most featuring Frank's wide-mouthed monkey mascot.

Cafés

Emporio Rulli

Stockton Street Pavilion, 333 Post St ⓣ415/433-1122. Café on Union Square's plaza that serves bracingly strong coffee and Italian pastries. There are tables outside if you want to lounge.

Mocca

175 Maiden Lane ⓣ415/956-1188. Small Italian café with plenty of outdoor seating; for around $7, sample a Mediterranean sandwich packed with tasty cured meats and pickles.

Morrow's Nut House

111 Geary St at Grant ⓣ415/362-7969. Tiny store selling nuts and candies and dried fruits by the piece or the pound – grab a healthy snack to go.

Sears Fine Food

439 Powell St at Post ⓣ415/986-1160. Daily 6.30am–2.30pm. Classic breakfast joint with a hearty, old-fashioned ambience: try the plate of eighteen tiny Swedish pancakes.

Yank Sing

427 Battery St at Clay ⓣ415/781-1111. The waitstaff at this dim sum house can almost always find a spot for you in the seemingly endless warren of dining rooms (even during the lunch hour, when they're routinely packed): ask for the onion cakes, which aren't on the trolley but are a house specialty.

Restaurants

Anjou

44 Campton Place at Stockton ⓣ415/392-5373. French bistro that's great for a bargain-priced prix-fixe lunch menu: soup or salad, plus an entree for $12.50.

Asia de Cuba

inside the *Clift Hotel*, 495 Geary St at Taylor ⓣ415/923-2300. Sino-Cuban fusion food in a funky setting, combining the freshness of Chinese cooking with the plentifulness of Cuban cuisine. The food's served family-style in huge portions and delivered dish by dish as soon as it's ready: try the tuna tartare on wonton crisps. Pricey (expect to spend at least $50 a head) but a treat, nonetheless.

Borobudur

700 Post St at Jones ⓣ415/775-1512. Smallish Indonesian restaurant, serving thick, tasty curries at budget prices – just come early to avoid the karaoke.

▲ St. francis hotel

Farallon

450 Post St at Powell ⓣ415/956-6969. The decor here is designed to resemble an underwater fantasy world – a pity that the jellyfish chandeliers are so offputting, since the food, including champagne-steamed clams and tuna carpaccio, is delicious. Entrees cost around $20.

Kokkari Estiatorio

200 Jackson St at Front ⓣ415/981-0983. Though this restaurant's look is pure Northern California, the moderately priced cuisine is classic Greek, especially the mouthwatering moussaka.

MarketBar

inside the Ferry Building ⓣ415/434-1100. The hearty food at this Ferry Building restaurant/bar is mostly Mediterranean (think seafood stew and herbed roast chicken). There's also an ample, interesting wine list if you just want to sip and stare at the passersby from an outdoor table.

Millennium

inside the *Savoy Hotel*, 580 Geary St at Hyde ⓣ415/345-3900, ⓦwww.millenniumrestaurant.com. Legendary vegetarian restaurant, offering flavor-packed entrees ($18–21), like fried portobello mushrooms, robust enough to please even avid meat eaters. The dark wood-paneled decor's gauzy and romantic, and the crowd's as much opera buff as eco-warrior.

Slanted Door

inside the Ferry Building ⓦwww.slanteddoor.com. French-Vietnamese restaurant that recently abandoned its long-term digs in the Mission for new premises at the Ferry Building: the food on the daily changing menu remains as delicious as ever, especially the grilled five-spice chicken and eclectic tea list. Lunchtime entrees cost $12–14, while at dinner the range is $17–22.

Bars

Carnelian Room

555 California St at Kearny ⓣ415/431-7500. Fifty-two floors up in the Bank of America Building, this elegant rooftop cocktail lounge has fantastic views of North Beach, Alcatraz, and the Transamerica Pyramid, especially at sunset. It's reached by an express elevator from the basement of the skyscraper.

Ferry Plaza Wine Merchant

inside the Ferry Building ⊕415/391-9400, ⊛www.fpwm.com. You can sample one of the many available intriguing vintages before you buy, all for around $7 a glass, in the twenty-seater Taster Bar here. There are selections from California as well as lesser known German, French, and Italian vineyards.

Ginger's Trois

246 Kearny St at Bush ⊕415/989-0282. A charming, low-rent gay bar smack in the heart of downtown; the bartenders sometimes play singalong showtunes on the piano.

Grandviews Lounge

inside the *Grand Hyatt*, 345 Stockton St at Sutter ⊕415/403-4847. This bar, 36 stories in the air, has fantastic north-facing views, allowing you to scope out Coit Tower and Alcatraz. Live jazz most evenings with no cover.

Harry Denton's Starlight Room

inside the *Sir Francis Drake Hotel*, 450 Powell St at Sutter ⊕415/395-8595. Dress up and drink martinis while swaying to live music from the Starlight Orchestra at this famous watering hole.

Red Room

inside the *Commodore International Hotel*, 827 Sutter St at Jones ⊕415/346-7666. This trendy, sexy bar is – as its name implies – completely red: walls, furniture, glasses, and even many of the drinks. The crowd's youngish and mixed.

The Redwood Room

inside the *Clift Hotel*, 495 Geary St at Taylor ⊕415/775-4700. Clubby, landmark drinking hole that was recently given a postmodern makeover by Philippe Starck: the freakish lightboxes on the wall display paintings that shift and fade – pity the drink prices are so outrageous.

Tunnel Top

601 Bush St at Stockton ⊕415/986-8900. Funky dive bar on top of the Stockton Street Tunnel, with industrial decor (a chandelier made from wine bottles is the centerpiece) and a hip, artsy crowd.

Performing arts and film

American Conservatory Theater (ACT)

Geary Theater, 415 Geary St at Taylor ⊕415/742-2228, ⊛www.act-sfbay.org. This is the Bay Area's resident leading theater group, known for its inventive staging (recent seasons have included *Waiting for Godot* and *Les Liaisons Dangereuses*). Tickets start at around $20.

Landmark's Embarcadero Cinema

1 Embarcadero Center at Sansome ⊕415/352-0810. Beautifully situated close to the water's edge, this is the only arthouse multiplex downtown, showing offbeat indies and Oscar-chasing dramas.

Post Street Theatre

450 Post St at Powell ⊕415/433-9500, ⊛www.450poststreet.com. Converted neo-Gothic theater, mostly housing mainstream crowd pleasers – whether musicals or Neil Simon-style stage sitcoms and dramas. Tickets from $50.

Chinatown and Jackson Square

San Francisco, with its throbbing, noisy Chinatown, is home to the second-largest Chinese community outside Asia (only New York City bests it). The neighborhood has its roots in the mostly Cantonese laborers who migrated there after the completion of the transcontinental railroad. A rip-roaring prostitution and gambling quarter (controlled by gangs, or tongs) developed during the nineteenth century but faded after World War II. The energy and crowds remain today, but it's touristy as opposed to seedy as people come to sample dim sum at one of the dozens of restaurants or buy a cheap souvenir from one of the throngs of nearly identical shops. Nearby Jackson Square is a studied contrast, a flash-frozen glimpse of nineteenth-century San Francisco, ghostly and evocative and now mostly home to upscale interior designers' showrooms.

Grant Avenue

Grant Avenue is Chinatown's main north-south artery, lined with gold-ornamented portals, brightly painted balconies, and some of the tackiest stores and facades in the city. One of the oldest thoroughfares in the city, it

was originally a wicked ensemble of opium dens, bordellos, and gambling huts known as DuPont Street and policed – if not terrorized – by *tong* hatchet men. The road was renamed in honor of civil war hero Ulysses S. Grant after the 1906 fire.

The gate that caps the avenue on the south end at Bush Street was a gift from the People's Republic of China to the city in 1969. It faces south, per *feng shui* precepts, and the four-character inscription reads *Xia tian wei gong*, or "The reason to exist is to serve the public good."

Grant is at its least tourist-tacky on the stretch just south of Columbus; but to best sample everyday life in Chinatown head to souvenir-stall-free Stockton Street, the commercial strip where most locals shop for groceries.

Waverley Place

This tiny backstreet was once the heart of Chinatown's extensive network of brothels, but is now known for a couple of opulent but out-of-sight temples. The namesake deity of **Norras temple** (third floor, no. 149) was the first lama from Tibet to teach high-level Buddhism in China; the chatty custodians will happily share stories. Meanwhile, **Tien Hou** (pronounced TEE-en How) **temple** (fourth floor, no. 125) commemorates the Taoist Goddess of Heaven; this is a more formal affair than the Norras temple, with gaudier decorations and a ceiling dripping with red tasseled lanterns. Note the tiny mirrors fastened to the balcony of 829 Sacramento St, at the eastern end of Waverly Place: they're designed to ward off evil spirits.

Portsmouth Square

Though it's now an outpost of Chinatown, filled with temple-like structures and older Chinese locals practicing *t'ai chi* or playing rowdy games of chess, Portsmouth Square (Washington Street and Grant Avenue) is in fact the site of the oldest European settlement in San Francisco. An English adventurer named William Richardson petitioned the Mexican government in 1835 for permission to establish a trading post here, which he called Yerba

▼ STOCKTON STREET

Buena after the sweet mint-like plant that local Native Americans stewed into tea. Eleven years later, when American sailors came ashore to claim the colony for the United States, they raised their flag in the small square at the center of Richardson's hamlet – look for the pennant flying today that marks the spot.

The best time to come here is on Saturday evening from spring through autumn (6–11pm), when a **night market** animates the square with performances of classical opera and traditional music surrounded by stalls selling everything from fresh honey to leather jackets; undeniably hokey, but lively fun.

Bank of Canton

743 Washington St at Grant Ave ⓣ415/421-5215. This small, red, pagoda-inspired building was thrown up in 1909 to house the Chinese-American Telephone Exchange: note how the roof curves out and then back on itself to foil evil spirits (they can only travel in a straight line, apparently). This was also the site of the offices of the *California Star* newspaper, which carried the news of the earliest ore discoveries back to the East Coast in 1848 and so breathlessly hyped the Gold Rush.

Jackson Square

Jackson Square Historic District (bordered by Washington, Columbus, Sansome, and Pacific streets), a cluster of Victorian buildings that survived the 1906 earthquake and fire, is a charming anomaly. The winding brickwork, hitching posts, and antique lamps of nearby **Hotaling Place**, running for a block south from Jackson Street, are an evocative time capsule of nineteenth-century San Francisco. Despite their obvious architectural charm, the restored red-brick houses owe their survival to prosaic rather than poetic reasons: the area was doused in water to ensure that 5000 barrels of highly flammable whiskey (stashed in the Hotaling Building, 451–455 Jackson St) didn't catch fire. It's not surprising that whiskey was stored in such large amounts here: Jackson Square, then known as the **Barbary Coast**, was San Francisco's answer to New York's Five Points: a decadent district full of brothels, bars, and vaudeville houses; though little evidence remains these days of the district's sordid history. Although a nice enough place to stroll around, today it's mostly choked with upscale interior-design studios.

▲ BANK OF CANTON

Shops

Ellison Herb Shop

805 Stockton St at Sacramento. The best-stocked herbal pharmacy in Chinatown, where you'll find clerks filling orders the ancient Chinese way – with hand-held scales and abaci – from drug cases filled with dried bark, shark fins, cicadas, ginseng, and other staples.

▲ CHINATOWN GATES

Cafés and snacks

Café de la Presse

352 Grant Ave at Bush ☎415/398-2680. Francophile café that's a great place to linger over a tasty, if pricey, coffee and a slice of the housemade *tarte tatin*.

Cityview Restaurant

662 Commercial St at Kearny ☎415/398-2838. Fresh, delicious dim sum restaurant that's both clean and calm, especially when the Financial District empties out at the weekend. The wide noodles with beef are outstanding.

Hang Ah Tea Room

1 Pagoda Place, off Sacramento St at Stockton ☎415/982-5686. Fri & Sat until 1am. Tasty neighborhood dim sum eatery with two major pluses – it's open late and prices are low ($5 for a rice plate, $2 for dim sum).

Il Massimo del Panino

441 Washington St at Sansome ☎415/834-0290. Unsurprisingly, given that it's next door to the Instituto Italiano di Cultura, this panini shop serves authentic pressed sandwiches and salads – fortunately, they're delicious, as well.

Imperial Tea Court

1411 Powell St at Broadway ☎415/788-6080. Steep yourself in the ambience of an old-world teahouse worthy of the last emperor: a peaceful bolthole amid the craziness of Chinatown – try the Jade Fire blend tea.

Lichee Garden

1416 Powell St at Broadway ☎415/397-2290. Classy dim sum restaurant filled with potted plants and carved wall hangings that buzzes with Chinese locals of all ages.

Mee Mee Bakery

1328 Stockton St at Broadway ☎415/362-3204. Little-known gem that serves delicate almondy treats as well as a variety of fortune cookies.

Restaurants

Bix

56 Gold St at Montgomery ⓣ415/433-6300, ⓦwww.bixrestaurant.com. Named after 1930s jazz cornetist Bix Beiderbecke, this high-end supper club has live music every night and no cover. The food's modern American, but it's the martinis and retro ambience that are the real draws.

The Globe

290 Pacific Ave at Battery ⓣ415/391-4132. The best place to grab dinner after hours alongside the waiters who flock here once their shift's ended – dinner's served until 1am and includes meat and fish entrees like grilled *bistecca* or shrimp baked in a wood oven (most cost $18–21).

Great Eastern

649 Jackson St at Kearny ⓣ415/986-2500. Located behind an impressive pagoda facade, this rather elegant, traditional Chinese restaurant specializes in seafood dishes like an excellent turtle soup. Prices are swankier than many of the other nearby restaurants (entrees around $15) but then again, so's the decor.

▲ sam wo

House of Nanking

919 Kearny St at Jackson ⓣ415/421-1429. Tiny, legendary restaurant – expect a long line (which will move faster than you expect), grumpy service, and a fabulous, underpriced meal of Chinese standards like Shanghai dumplings ($5.95).

Lucky Creation

854 Washington St at Waverly ⓣ415/989-0818. Budget all-vegetarian option, with imaginative faux-meat dishes created from tofu and wheat gluten that's been chopped and shaped so that it can even look like a cutlet or wing.

Plouf

40 Belden Lane at Bush ⓣ415/986-6491. Yuppie-thronged French bistro, serving mostly seafood – including ten different kinds of mussels – for $12–16/dish; the best place to sit is one of the outdoor tables.

Sam Wo

813 Washington St at Grant ⓣ415/982-0596. Mon–Sat until 3am. Popular late-night spot where Kerouac, Ginsberg, and others used to hold court – expect very cheap but mediocre food, brusque service, and lashings of atmosphere.

Yuet Lee

1300 Stockton St at Broadway ⓣ415/982-6020. Daily until 3am. Easily spotted thanks to its garish green exterior, this pricey diner has on-site fish tanks, so you know the seafood is fresh – try steamed fish or clams with black bean sauce, or a bowl of steamed frogs for the brave ($18).

Bars

The Bubble Lounge

714 Montgomery St at Columbus ⓣ415/434-4204. Champagne bar that attracts a young, gussied, and Gucci'd-up crowd with its surprisingly reasonable prices.

Buddha Bar

901 Grant Ave at Washington ⓣ415/362-1792. Darkish bar that feels far removed from urban America, filled with older locals slapping down *mah jong* tiles.

Cathay House

718 California St at Grant ⓣ415/982-3388. There's an inviting circular bar at the center of this so-so restaurant, presided over by a massive statue of Buddha.

Li Po's Bar

916 Grant Ave at Jackson ⓣ415/982-0072. Named after the Chinese poet, this raucous and kitschy bar is something of a literary hangout among Chinatown regulars: try and bag one of the red booths at the back.

Clubs and live music

Clarion Music Center

816 Sacramento St at Grant ⓣ415/391-1317, ⓦwww.clarionmusic.com. A cozy little theater with a schedule of local and touring world music bands, who usually play on Fridays at 8pm. Cover is usually $5.

▼ DUCKS FOR SALE

North Beach

Inland North Beach is a sunny neighborhood sitting in a valley sheltered by several hills, and is known as the hub of San Francisco's Italian community (for the record, the area was named while still on the waterfront, before landfill extended the peninsula). The freewheeling European atmosphere here made the area attractive to 1950s Beat writers, who helped turn San Francisco into a beacon for later counterculturalists like the hippies and flower children. Today, though the Beats are long gone and North Beach is thoroughly gentrified, it still retains a pungent enough Italian flavor to draw hungry or nostalgic tourists to walk its streets or hang out in one of the legendary cafés – and any espresso served here puts Starbucks to shame. Most of the sights and facilities jostle together along Columbus Avenue, the main drag that marks the boundary between North Beach here and Chinatown to the west.

City Lights Bookstore

261 Columbus Ave at Broadway ⓣ415/362-8193, ⓦwww.citylights.com. An independent bookstore that was the heart of Beat North Beach, *City Lights* still fights on today under original owner Lawrence Ferlinghetti, now well into his eighties. Ferlinghetti was an early advocate and publisher of the **Beats**, the loose writers' collective that included Jack Kerouac and Allen Ginsberg, based in North Beach and whose

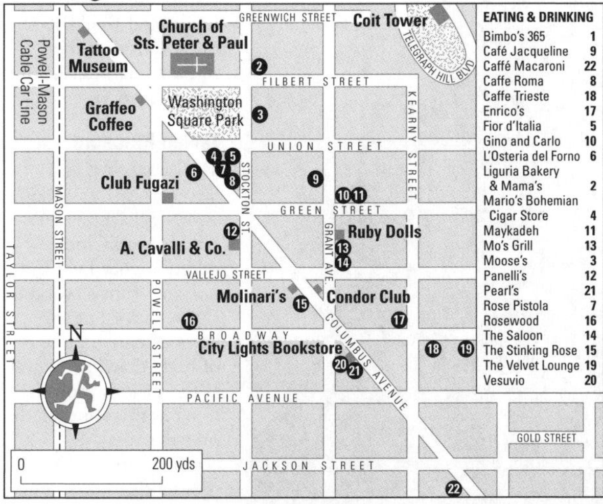

bohemian lifestyle was the *succès de scandale* of the 1950s. The best reason to stop by *City Lights* – aside from experiencing its astonishingly grumpy staff first hand – is the upstairs poetry room, well stocked with not only Beat masterworks but also lesser-known modern verse.

Condor Club

300 Columbus Ave at Broadway ⓣ415/781-8222. Though now a nondescript sports bar, this was once the site of the notorious *Condor Club*, where, in 1964, server Carol "44 inches" Doda slipped out of her top and into the history books by becoming the first-ever topless waitress. Look for the neon nipples sign that's been preserved by the current owners.

▼ condor club

Washington Square Park

This grassy plaza with ample benches is the soul of North Beach, serving as a playground for local children as well as a workout studio for older Chinese locals, who appear each morning in scattered groups and silently practice *t'ai chi*. The beefy bronze statue on its western edge was donated by Lillie Coit, a wealthy but wacky woman who was obsessed with firemen and honored them with both this smallish monument and the massive tower on Telegraph Hill (see p.87).

Church of Saints Peter and Paul

660 Filbert St at Columbus ⓣ415/421-5219, ⓦwww.stspeterpaul.san-francisco.ca.us. The white lacy spires of this church look like a pair of picturesque fairytale castle towers. Although it's seen as the spiritual home of the local Italian community, the church also now offers Masses in Cantonese, as well as Italian and English, in order to reflect the shifting character of the neighborhood.

Tattoo Museum

841 Columbus Ave at Greenwich ⓣ415/775-4991, ⓦwww.lyletuttle.com. Free. At this quirky local oddity, owner Lyle Tuttle not only runs a working tattoo parlor but also hosts extensive displays of body drawings as well as the various tools used to paint them into flesh over the years – certainly not for the squeamish.

▲ VOLUNTEER FIREMAN MEMORIAL

Shops

A. Cavaili & Co

1441 Stockton St at Columbus ☎415/421-4219. Italian-language bookstore with magazines, books, and movies.

Graffeo Coffee

733 Columbus Ave at Filbert ☎415/986-2420, ⓦwww.graffeo.com. There are huge sacks of coffee piled up all over this store, where the Repetto family has been roasting coffee for more than sixty years.

Molinari's

373 Columbus Ave at Vallejo ☎415/421-2337. North Beach deli/grocery jammed to the rafters with Italian goodies – buy a hunk of parmesan to take home.

Ruby Dolls

1318 Grant Ave at Vallejo ☎415/834-9762. Funky fantasy and fetish wear for brave women.

Cafés and snacks

Caffe Roma

526 Columbus Ave at Union ☎415/296-7942. The owners roast their own coffee on the premises and serve a killer cappuccino. The flaky Italian pastries aren't bad either.

Caffe Trieste

601 Vallejo St at Grant ☎415/392-6739. Small, crowded Italian coffeehouse noted for its Saturday afternoon amateur opera hour and where Francis Ford Coppola is rumored to have scribbled out the script for *The Godfather*.

Liguria Bakery

1700 Stockton St at Filbert ☎415/421-3786. Old-world Italian bakery selling fresh focaccia – get there at least by noon as it closes once they're sold out.

Mama's

1701 Stockton St at Washington Square ☎415/362-6421. Tues–Sun 8am–3pm. Hands down one of the best brunches in the city – try the crab benedict or a gooey serving of French toast. There are certain to be massive lines at the weekend, but it's well worth the wait.

Mario's Bohemian Cigar Store

566 Columbus Ave at Union ☎415/362-0536. No cigars anymore but the café still serves good coffee and chunky, cheap sandwiches.

▲ mario's bohemian cigar store

Mo's Grill

1322 Grant Ave at Vallejo ☎415/788-3779. Thick, juicy hamburgers in a no-fuss, no-frills diner where the fresh ground beef is charred to order on a fiery grill.

Panelli's

1419 Stockton St at Columbus ☎415/421-2541. Old school Italian sandwich shop serving meaty, enormous sandwiches for around $7 each.

Restaurants

Café Jacqueline

1454 Grant Ave at Green ☎415/981-5565. It's all soufflés, all the time at this romantic, candlelit restaurant, whether savory or sweet – the strawberry is especially fresh and superb. Book ahead, but expect to pay for the privilege.

Caffé Macaroni

59 Columbus Ave at Jackson ☎415/956-9737. Tiny, intimate date restaurant that serves well-made antipasti and main courses including buttery plates of gnocchi at close to budget prices – don't worry if the tiny, streetside room looks too full, as there's extra seating upstairs.

Enrico's

504 Broadway at Kearny ☎415/982-6223, ⓦwww.enricossidewalkcafe.com. A Cal-Italian staple serving good, simple food (entrees $17–23) and featuring a streetside patio that's handy for smokers. Try the housemade lasagne.

Fior d'Italia

601 Union St at Stockton ☎415/986-1886, ⓦwww.fior.com. *Fior* maintains a deliberately old-fashioned aura thanks to its bow-tied waiters (after all, it claims to be the oldest Italian restaurant in America). The

menu's mostly robust, rich pastas at reasonable prices.

L'Osteria del Forno

519 Columbus Ave at Green ⓣ415/982-1124. Gloriously authentic Italian gem that's one of the best restaurants in the area, with a small, market-driven menu – try the roast pork braised in milk if it's available – and priced in a wallet-friendly fashion.

Maykadeh

470 Green St at Grant ⓣ415/362-8286. Low-key Persian eatery that's a great option for budget-conscious vegetarians – try the *khoresht bamejan* (tomato and eggplant stew).

Moose's

1652 Stockton St at Filbert ⓣ415/989-7800, ⓦwww.mooses.com. At this standout American brasserie, the food (entrees $18–25), like polenta with gorgonzola and homemade sausage, is tastier and more adventurous and sophisticated than you might expect, given the blandish decor.

Rose Pistola

532 Columbus Ave at Green ⓣ415/399-0499. Restaurant/bar offering flavorful California-style Italian antipasti: ideal if you want to sit on a barstool, sip a glass of wine, and graze on a few snacks (appetizers are $8–10, entrees around $20).

The Stinking Rose

325 Columbus Ave at Broadway ⓣ415/781-7673, ⓦwww.thestinkingrose.com. If you're fond of their gimmick, you'll leave happy – at this local oddity every dish, even the desserts, features garlic as its prime ingredient. The gnocchi in garlic-brie sauce ($12) is a standout, and you can't leave here without trying the garlic ice cream ($2) for dessert.

Bars

Gino and Carlo

548 Green St at Grant ⓣ415/421-0896. Classic pub aimed at hardened barflies, open at 6am for shiftworkers on their way home and filled with old-school locals all day.

Rosewood

732 Broadway at Powell ⓣ415/951-4886. There's no sign outside this retro groovy bar, known for killer cocktails and loungecore DJs – avoid the weekends, unless you want to join the crush of out-of-towners on the sidewalk waiting to get in.

▼ the stinking rose

The Saloon

1232 Grant Ave at Vallejo ⓣ415/989-7666. Gritty bar that's stood for more than a hundred years (and it shows) – not the plushest place, but ideal if you want to soak up raucous blues and stock up on cheap booze. No cover.

Spec's Adler Museum Café

12 Saroyan Place at Columbus ⓣ415/421-4112. Friendly dive bar in the heart of North Beach, where an older, eccentric local crowd hangs out with the chatty barstaff.

Vesuvio

255 Columbus Ave at Broadway ⓣ415/362-3370, ⓦwww.vesuvio.com. The interior of this famed Beat haunt looks like an explosion in a scrapbook factory – the walls are covered with collages and photos. It's friendly and low key, and despite its historic reputation there are equal numbers of tourists and locals propping up the bar.

Performing arts and film

Beach Blanket Babylon at Club Fugazi

678 Green St at Powell ⓣ415/421-4222, ⓦwww.beachblanketbabylon.com. Unmissable local theatrical institution, a lampooning revue that's like *Saturday Night Live* with better and bigger wigs. Based loosely on Snow White's quest to find a man, the quick-fire humor and charm of the mostly veteran performers guarantees a riotous evening – it doesn't hurt that drinks are served, either. Tickets $20–70; 21 and over only.

Clubs and live music

Bimbo's 365 Club

1025 Columbus at Chestnut ⓣ415/474-0365, ⓦwww.bimbos365.com. This traditional 1940s supper club offers more than just Frank Sinatra tribute bands, thanks to a savvy booker who also schedules underground European acts. $20 and up.

▲ vesuvio

Jazz at Pearl's

256 Columbus at Broadway ⓣ415/291-8255. Nightly sets by a rotating cast of regulars, many of whom have gigged with the biggest names around. $5 weekdays for 9pm, $10 weekends; closed Sun.

The Velvet Lounge

443 Broadway at Montgomery ⓣ415/788-0228, ⓦwww.thevelvetlounge.com. Dressy, mainstream bar/club with DJs and live music most nights – fun, if a bit of a meat market at weekends. Fri–Sat $10.

Nob Hill, Russian Hill, and Telegraph Hill

These three hills are the highest points in the center of the city, so make sure to wear comfortable shoes while exploring. Telegraph Hill (named after an old communications station that once stood here) holds a quiet cluster of hill-hugging homes that cascade down to the waterfront on its eastern edge. Upscale Russian Hill (named after six unknown Russian sailors buried here in the early 1800s) is largely residential, its summit capped by a few modest high-rise apartment buildings; it's served by a chic strip of shops and cafés along upper Polk Street and most often visited for those looking to take a white-knuckle ride down twisty Lombard Street. And Nob Hill (whose moniker comes from the rich industrial "nabobs" who settled here in the late nineteenth century after the cable car made it residentially accessible) is the snootiest of all – hushed and wealthy, with few attractions other than its multimillion-dollar homes.

Coit Tower

☎415/362-0808, Ⓦwww.coittower.org. Daily 10am–6pm. $3. Loopy local eccentric Lillie Coit was obsessed with firemen and spent her life hanging out at firemen's balls and playing poker with her firefighting buddies. On her death in 1929, Lillie left a chunk of her sizable fortune to build a monument to the brave heroes; the phallic, firehose-inspired concrete Coit Tower at the peak of Telegraph Hill was the result. You can ascend the 212ft column for impressive views across the city, provided there isn't too much fog. Otherwise, it's still worth trekking up the hill just to enjoy the well-preserved frescoes that decorate the interior of the tower's base, executed by students of the Mexican communist artist **Diego Rivera**. The intense, somber WPA murals were highly controversial and branded left wing when unveiled – they certainly reflect the preoccupations of the Depression era (work, work, and more work), though it's ironic that the few women seen are either shopping or picking flowers on a farm. Note Raymond Bertrand's *Meat*

▼ FILBERT STEPS

Industry, in which the artist cleverly adapts the building's windows to his scene as sausage smokers. The most direct path up the hill is on its western side along Filbert Street – a steepish ten-minute climb with good views on the way.

Filbert and Greenwich steps

The eastern face of Telegraph Hill is a rustic, idyllic enclave of low-slung old houses hidden behind leafy, overhanging gardens. No wonder the simple cottages (some of them built in the 1850s by Gold Rushers) here have skyrocketed in value in recent years – the views across the Bay are astonishing. You can best enjoy them by descending on foot eastward down from the summit, through the crisscrossing maze-like walkways that are etched into the side of the hill and connect the clusters of homes. The best-known routes are the Greenwich Steps, which cling to the hill at a 45-degree angle, and the Filbert Steps, surrounded by a handful of simple houses that were built by 1850s Gold Rush immigrants and somehow survived the 1906 fire. The other notable roadway on this side of Telegraph Hill is tiny Napier Lane, famous as one of the last boardwalk streets in San Francisco and lined with bucolic cottages.

Levi Strauss Visitor Center

Levi's Plaza, 1155 Battery Street at Filbert ☎415/501-6000, Ⓦwww.levistrauss.com. Mon–Fri 9am–6pm, Sat–Sun 10am–5pm. Free. The ugly brick office complex here is the world HQ for Levi Strauss, the local jean genius who made a fortune making miners' pants in the Gold Rush. The company's recently opened a flashy new visitors' center to showcase its history and product. It's a fun, if inevitably a little breathless, collection, though the display of consumers' letters to the company is intriguing, as is the chance to catch a screening of many of its past TV ads.

San Francisco Art Institute

800 Chestnut St at Leavenworth ⓣ415/771-7020, ⓦwww.sanfranciscoart.edu. This low-rise Mission-style building, a working school whose alumni include Jerry Garcia, clings to the side of a steep street on Russian Hill. It's easy to miss, but make sure to seek out the institute's one notable artwork in the Diego Rivera Gallery where there's an outstanding, muscular mural by the artist. *The Making of a Fresco Showing the Building of a City* was executed in 1931 when he was at the height of his fame. Rivera's the chubby, dark-haired figure with his back to the viewer in the center of the painting.

Lombard Street

Russian Hill's Lombard Street is famed as San Francisco's twistiest street and looks like a terracotta-tiled waterchute for cars. With eight tight curves between Hyde and Leavenworth, there's a 5mph speed limit – not that you'll be able to drive much faster given how many others are usually there to enjoy the drive – but you can also pick your way down on foot via the stepped sidewalk. The best time to enjoy it is early morning or, better still, late at night when the city lights twinkle below and the tourists have gone; photographs are more impressive taken from the foot, rather than the summit, of the hill.

Cable Car Museum

1201 Mason St at Washington ⓣ415/474-1997, ⓦwww.cablecarmuseum.com. Essentially an indoor viewing platform for the innards of the system's engineering, rather than a resting home for retired carriages, this Nob Hill museum is a worthwhile stop thanks to the informative placards that will help even the least mechanically minded understand how cable cars work. The gift shop's also a fine place for fun souvenirs.

Grace Cathedral

1100 California St at Jones ⓦwww.gracecathedral.org. Episcopal Grace Cathedral is one of the biggest hulks of neo-Gothic architecture in the US. A rather bland and disappointing copy of Notre Dame in Paris, it was begun after the 1906 fire but took until the early 1960s to finish – a fact sadly evident in its hodgepodge of poured concrete styles. The cathedral's notable for three things: first, that George W. Bush's ancestor Godwin was pastor here for a while; second, for the copies of Ghiberti's Renaissance-inducing doors from the Florence Baptistry on its main entrance, included for no reason other than that they were available to the architect; and finally, for the cozy AIDS

▼ LOMBARD STREET

▲ GRACE CATHEDRAL AIDS CHAPEL

Interfaith Chapel with its vibrant cast-bronze altarpiece by the late pop artist Keith Haring.

Shops

ab fits

1519 Grant Ave at Union ⓣ415/982-5726, ⓦwww.abfits.substation.com. Imaginative men's and women's boutique offering directional casual and jeanswear from the likes of Rogan, J. Lindeberg, SBU, and Seven at moderate prices.

Cris

2056 Polk St at Broadway ⓣ415/474-1191. High-end consignment store, crammed with pristine designer garments from recent seasons at reasonable prices for men and women.

Les Cent Culottes

1504 Vallejo St at Polk ⓣ415/614-2586, ⓦwww.lescentculottes.com. The name of this all-French lingerie store means "100 Panties" – it's the place to come for upscale women's underwear, whether skimpy or supportive.

Old Vogue

1412 Grant Ave at Green ⓣ415/392-1522. Pricey vintage store with a wide men's selection and piles of good-as-new jeans on the upper mezzanine.

Cafés

Boulangerie de Polk

2310 Polk St at Green ⓣ415/345-1107. Tues–Sat 7am–7pm, Sun to 6pm. Flaky croissants and crusty breads are the specialty at this new French bakery – there are a few seats if you want to sit and eat.

Il Fornaio

1265 Battery St at Greenwich Hill ⓣ415/986-0100. Italian bakery that makes flavorful sandwiches with homemade bread either to go or to linger over on its shady patio.

Restaurants

Fog City Diner

1300 Battery St at Filbert ⓣ415/982-2000, ⓦwww.fogcitydiner.com. Upscale, retro diner with Art Deco-ish fixtures, offering quirky tweaks on traditional recipes like mascarpone brioche French toast and chicken hash with lobster (more succulent than it sounds).

Matterhorn

2323 Van Ness Ave at Green ⓣ415/885-6116. Hidden in an apartment building, this authentically Swiss restaurant (the kitschy ski lodge-style decor was shipped here in pieces from the motherland) is known for its fondues, whether cheese, beef, or chocolate. The standout's undeniably the Fondue Ticinese, a thick and spicy blend of cheeses, pepperoncini, and tomatoes.

▼ MARK HOPKINS INTER-CONTINENTAL

Okoze Sushi Bar

1207 Union St at Hyde ⓣ415/567-3397. Chi-chi sushi bar with a sleek interior (think bamboo and muted green) and a funky menu offering locally named dishes like Russian Hill rainbow rolls, with nori, salmon, and tuna; and Hyde Rail Track rolls, which features soy beans.

Petit Robert

2300 Polk St at Green ⓣ415/922-8100. Atmospheric French bistro offering mostly tapas-style *petits plats* for $5–14.50 – the steak tartare is superb.

Piperade

1015 Battery St at Green ⓣ415/391-2555, ⓦwww.piperade.com. Basque restaurant with rustic, wooden tables and a robust menu including cod in smoky broth and the namesake, ratatouille-esque stew; entrees cost $15–17. The warm atmosphere and the affable, attentive service are big plusses.

Sushi Groove

1916 Hyde St at Union ⓣ415/440-1905. Groovy, throbbing modern sushi restaurant offering quirky maki roll combinations and unmissable sake martinis, all to a background of loud house music. Shame about the sloppy service.

Tablespoon

2209 Polk St at Vallejo ⓣ415/268-0140. Pricey fusion restaurant, combining American, French, and Asian influences (pork tenderloin or offbeat Hawaiian fish at $17–20 per plate, for example). Make sure to try one of their housemade wine mojitos and to save room for desserts like rhubarb soup or roast grape and pistacho pizza.

Yabbie's Coastal Kitchen

2237 Polk St at Green ⓣ415/474-4088. Shellfish of every variety served in every way imaginable – though the prices are as high as the quality – in an old-fashioned setting; oysters chilled on the half shell are the specialty.

Bars

1550 Hyde Café and Wine Bar

1550 Hyde St at Jackson ⓣ415/775-1550, ⓔ1550hyde@earthlink.net. The menu here is organic and Mediterranean with a focus on local suppliers. The real draw, though, is its extensive wine list, with 26 different regional wines by the glass.

Pier 23

Pier 23 ⓣ415/362-5125. Sit out on the deck under the heatlamps and enjoy cocktails by the Bay, plus tasty Creole snacks. Thursday's a real scene, thanks to a raucous after-work crowd.

Tonga Room

inside the *Fairmont Hotel*, 950 Mason St at California ⓣ415/772-5278. Basement Tiki lounge with grass huts and a floating band at night, not to mention an indoor rainstorm every fifteen minutes.

Tonic

2360 Polk St at Green ⓣ415/771-5535. A happening little pick-up joint, dark and chic, serving cheap mixed drinks at a long mahogany bar.

Top of the Mark

inside the *Mark Hopkins Hotel*, 999 California St at Mason ⓣ415/392-3434, ⓦwww.markhopkins.net. The most famous of the city's rooftop bars, with sweeping views from the summit of Nob Hill, was founded in 1939 and still retains its old-world elegance. Try the trademark Top of the Mark cocktail – vodka and vermouth, served with a pickled green tomato. $5–10 cover for live music.

▼ TONGA ROOM

Fisherman's Wharf and Alcatraz

San Francisco's northern waterfront is dominated by the city's number-one-crowd puller, Fisherman's Wharf. Each year, millions of visitors plow through its overpriced commercial gimmickry for a glimpse of what remains of a nearly obsolete fishing industry (these days the few fishermen that can afford the exorbitant mooring charges are usually done with their work before visitors arrive). There's ultimately little that's appealing about this tourist magnet (aside from a number of admittedly excellent restaurants) with one major exception – Alcatraz, the fabled island prison and one of San Francisco's unmissable sights.

Fisherman's Wharf

Despite its tacky reputation, the wharf is a massively popular tourist destination (Piers 39, 41, 43, 43 1/2, and 45 Ⓦwww.fishermanswharf.org) – creative interpretation of statistics allows it to claim to be the most visited attraction anywhere in America. If you join the millions flocking to the waterfront, it's best to avoid weekends and try to stop by as early as possible before the tour buses take over. Amid the souvenir stands, hot dog carts, and tourist tackiness, there's one amusing exception: the freaky Bush Man. He can usually be found lurking, comically unhidden behind a bush

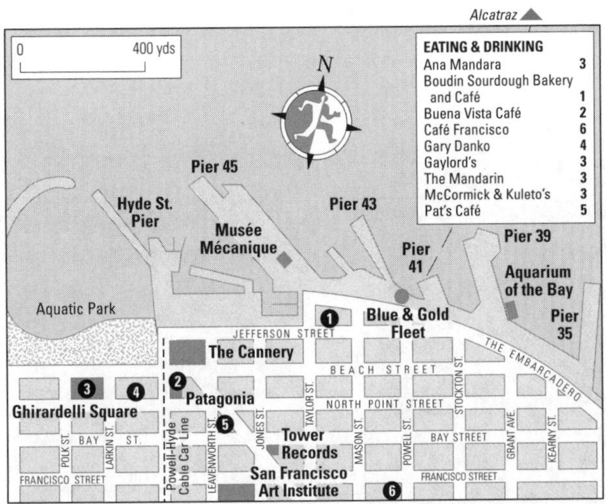

on a pole, on the walkway near Pier 43, leaping out periodically to startle passersby, who drop a steady stream of change into his bucket. As for that honking noise, it's a colony of adolescent male sea lions that's taken over the floating platforms at sea level between Piers 39 and 41; they're protected by the Marine Mammal Act and so are free to come and go as they please – just make sure not to feed them, as that's illegal.

Ghirardelli Square

900 N Point St at Larkin ⓣ415/775-5500, ⓦwww.ghirardellisq.com. Marking the western edge of Fisherman's Wharf, Ghirardelli Square is one of two old factories in the area that have been converted into boutiquey malls (The Cannery, 2801 Leavenworth St at Jefferson, is the other). Now housing a bland selection of stores alongside some surprisingly good restaurants, it was originally the headquarters of failed 49er and candy magnate Domenico Ghirardelli, who first discovered how to sweat the butter from raw cocoa and revolutionized the chocolate-making industry – making himself a millionaire thanks to the brown gold.

Musée Mécanique

Pier 45 at Taylor St ⓣ415/346-2000, ⓦwww.museemecanique.com. Newly installed here after being evicted from its long-term home under Cliff House (see p.144), the Musée Mécanique, a collection of historic arcade games, may now be easier to reach but has lost a little of its careworn, tatty charm thanks to new, purpose-built digs. The games are the same as ever, mixing retro arcade classics like Pac Man with faux fortune tellers and the museum's best-known holding, a cackling clown. Entrance is free, but you'll need plenty of quarters to properly enjoy the games.

Aquarium of the Bay

Pier 39 at Beach and Stockton streets ⓣ888/732-3483, ⓦwww.aquariumofthebay.com; $12.95, $6.50 kids. Despite the stagey elevator ride that "dives" you to the bottom of the sea, the aquarium is still worth a visit thanks to the

▼ A VIEW OF FISHERMAN'S WHARF

▲ ALCATRAZ

spectacular close-up views of fish and crustaceans that surround you as you trundle slowly along a 400ft acrylic viewing tunnel. The other must-see (or do) is a petting pool where visitors can actually touch leopard sharks and bat rays.

Alcatraz

☎415/705-5555, Ⓦwww.nps.gov/alcatraz. The black, crusty island visible from the wharf is Alcatraz, nicknamed "The Rock." For the first half of the twentieth century, this twelve-acre islet was **America's most dreaded high-security prison** and home to brand-name criminals like Al Capone and Machine Gun Kelly. The Prison on the Rock was notorious for its isolation: though it's only 1.25 miles from the city, the six-knot current in the Bay is so fierce that even strong swimmers had no hope of successful escape (nine men tried, none succeeded). The government shut down the jail in 1963 for financial reasons; when it reopened as a tourist attraction a few years later, Alcatraz went from money pit to goldmine – now, 750,000 visitors pass through each year. As for the Rock's curious name, it's Spanglish from *alcatraces*, or pelicans, birds that were common in the Bay when the first European settlers arrived.

Once on the island, most people opt to use the hour-long self-guided **audio tours**, which provide sharp anecdotal commentary about life and events in the prison, mostly voiced by former inmates and guards. Skip the dull twelve-minute introductory film at the dock – if you want to learn more, join one of the lively, free ranger talks that run on a rolling schedule: the day's topics and times are marked on a whiteboard on the wall by the dock.

The island itself is surprisingly small up close, and the ramshackle cottages dotted around the main prison building make it look like an old Mediterranean fishing port – albeit plastered with blaring Federal signs. Once inside, though, it's easy to understand how emotionally grueling a stay on the Rock must have been – the bare cells are spartan and tiny, while the windowless isolation pens are pitch black once the door is closed.

Blue and Gold Fleet boats (Ⓣ415/773-1188, Ⓦwww.blueandgoldfleet.com; $13.25 with audio tour, $9.25 without) depart from Pier 41, beginning at 9.30am, last boat back at 4.30pm. The best boats to catch are the first, since the jail's not yet packed with other tourists when you arrive and will be evocatively empty; or the last, which offers a stunning view of the sunset in wintertime. Note that whatever boat you plan to catch, reservations are essential – book at least two weeks ahead in peak season, and about one week in advance during off-season.

▲ SEA LIONS ON FLOATING PLATFORMS

Shops

Patagonia

770 North Point Ⓣ415/771-2050. This store, with its functional performance clothing, could lay claim to being the patron saint of Bay Area outdoor enthusiasts. Prices are fair, and many products have more of a fashion sensibility than other sportswear stores.

Tower Records

2525 Jones St at Columbus Ave Ⓣ415/885-0500. Local megastore, with a huge classical annex across the street.

Cafés

Boudin Sourdough Bakery & Café

156 Jefferson St at Mason Ⓣ415/928-1849. The sandwiches here feature this chain's signature local sourdough bread, made using a 150-year-old recipe.

Café Francisco

2161 Powell St at Francisco Ⓣ415/397-2602. Cheap neighborhood café that's great for a lazy breakfast on a sunny day, especially when taken at one of the outdoor tables.

Pat's Café

2701 Leavenworth St at Columbus ⓣ415/776-8735. Bright and basic café with simple formica tables and a short menu of burgers and sandwiches, starting at $6.

Restaurants

Gary Danko

800 North Point at Hyde ⓣ415/749-2060, ⓦwww.garydanko.com. The poshest restaurant in San Francisco, serving an adventurous ever-changing American menu – it's definitely performance food, as each dish is unveiled from beneath a silver *cloche* with a determined flourish. At $74, the tasting menu is an unforgettable, if wallet-busting, experience.

Gaylord's

in Ghirardelli Square, 900 North Point St at Larkin ⓣ415/771-8822, ⓦwww.gaylords.com. Fine tandooris and curries in a lovely setting, several floors above the tumult of tourists – the express lunch deals ($12–15) are a good-value option.

The Mandarin

in Ghirardelli Square, 900 North Point ⓣ415/673-8812, ⓦwww.themandarin.com. Authentic, upscale Chinese food in a lush, hushed dining room – try the Kung Pao chicken ($11.95) or the surprisingly tender, tasty sweet & sour pork ($11.95).

McCormick and Kuleto's

in Ghirardelli Square, 900 North Point St at Larkin ⓣ415/929-1730, ⓦwww.mccormickandschmicks.com. Old-school fish restaurant that serves reliable, sometimes even exceptional, seafood: the salmon gravlax is delicious, as are the coconut prawns wth papaya mango salsa. Expect to pay around $20 per entrée.

Bars

Ana Mandara

in Ghirardelli Square, 891 Beach St at Polk ⓣ415/771-6800, ⓦwww.ana-mandara.com. The beautiful, bamboo-decorated lounge at this upscale restaurant is a soothing place to listen to live jazz and sip a cocktail.

▼ FOOD AT FISHERMAN'S WHARF

Buena Vista Café

2765 Hyde St at Beach ⓣ415/474-5044. The place that invented Irish coffee (or so they say) – try a whiskey-soaked, cream-topped cup or two at this divey pub and see how the original ranks against every other foamy boozy version you've tried.

Pacific Heights and the northern waterfront

Perched on steep hills, the millionaires' ghetto of Pacific Heights is home to some of the city's most monumental Victorian piles and stone mansions. The area's architectural uniformity is down to its late development, since the hilly terrain could only be colonized once gradient-conquering cable car lines had linked it to downtown. Close by, in the northern districts of the Marina and Cow Hollow, are the manicured haunts and well-appointed apartments of San Francisco's thrusting young professionals, as well as, not surprisingly, a good selection of upscale bars and restaurants. Immediately south of the Heights stands Japantown, an artificially created enclave that houses much of the city's sizable Japanese community. It's a terrific place, not only for cheap sushi but to browse for Asian art or pick up a Japanese pop CD or two.

Haas-Lilienthal House

2007 Franklin St at Washington ⓣ415/441-3004, ⓦwww.sfheritage.org. 1hr tours leave every 20–30min, Wed noon–3pm, Sun 11am–4pm. $5. An ornate double-size Queen Anne-style home that was built for his growing family by a wealthy merchant, William Haas, this house is a grand symbol of old wealth, with intricate wooden towers outside and Tiffany art-glass and stenciled leather paneling inside. It's worth stopping by to poke around the well-preserved interior, though the talky tours are more illuminating about the family's day-to-day life than about the architecture of the building, an eye-catching example of the city's Victorian style.

St Mary of the Assumption

1111 Gough St at Geary ⓣ415/567-2020, ⓦwww.stmarycathdralsf.org. Mon–Fri 7am–4.30pm, Sat 7am–6.30pm, Sun 7am–4.45pm. Built in 1971 to replace a fire-damaged predecessor, this stunning piece of modernist architecture in lower Pacific Heights has unfairly been derided by local wags for supposedly resembling a washing-machine agitator (thus its nickname, "Our Lady of the

▼ HAAS-LILIENTHAL HOUSE

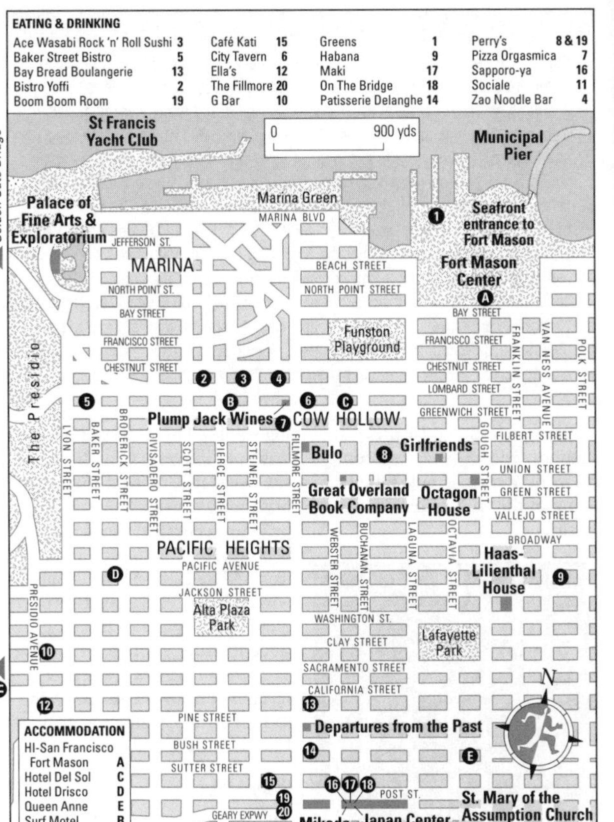

Maytag"). Make sure to stop inside to see its swooping, vaulted interior that seems to swirl with movement and the impressive organ that looks like a pin cushion with a Mohawk.

Japan Center

Post St between Fillmore and Laguna streets ⓣ415/922-6776. A sprawling shopping mall that was built in 1968 as a conciliatory gesture toward the local Japanese community – many of whom had, like other Japanese-Americans, been held in internment camps during World War II – and is now the center of a densely concentrated Japanese community of around 12,000 people who keep the food, record, and book stores here in brisk business. The major sight is the 100-foot **Peace Pagoda**, standing in the outdoor central plaza that links the main buildings and looks like a stack of poured concrete space-age mushrooms. Another peaceful refuge in the Center is the **Kabuki Hot Springs,** 1750 Geary Blvd at Fillmore (ⓣ415/922-6000, ⓦwww.kabukisprings.com), a

Victorians

Built in the second half of the nineteenth century from once-plentiful redwoods culled from the Marin headlands to the north, these fancy mansions fell out of popularity with the arrival of Art Deco in the 1920s, and many were demolished as part of the vogue for urban redevelopment in the 1960s. Those that survived – and there are around 13,500 Victorians in San Francisco proper – are now highly sought after by nostalgic (and wealthy) young homebuyers. There are three main styles: **Italianate**, marked out by the use of Corinthian columns; **Stick**, signaled by the decorative vertical "sticks" appliquéd to the facade; and **Queen Anne**, with roof gables and turrets. Note that the lurid color schemes with which they're so associated are an anachronism: originally painted entirely pale green or white, some Victorians took on their Technicolor hues when hippies, who'd moved into abandoned or unloved mansions in nearby Haight-Ashbury, were allowed to paint their homes psychedelic colors by grateful, money-saving landlords. Very quickly, houses across the city – even in conservative Pacific Heights – followed suit.

soothing traditional Japanese bathhouse that's been funked up by its new owners but still retains some of the spa's original eccentricity.

▲ PEACE PAGODA

Chestnut Street

The area known as the Marina, the motherlode for San Francisco's yuppie techie types, centers on **Chestnut Street**, a strip of shops, restaurants, and lounges that has a (deserved) reputation as a haven for swinging singles. The local watering holes are known as "high intensity breeder bars," and the neighborhood's massive Safeway has a pick-up scene that's so fierce it's been dubbed, without a trace of irony, "The Body Shop." The Marina's one of the least earthquake-proof parts of the city, since it's built entirely on landfill in an area that was artificially reclaimed from the sea in 1915 to house the Panama Pacific International Exhibition.

Union Street

This is the main artery through the district of Cow Hollow, which was once a small valley of pastures and dairies in the post-Gold Rush years (hence the name). The stretch between Van Ness and Divisadero holds one of the city's densest concentrations of boutiques and cafés; it buzzes with neighborhood shoppers, especially on weekends, and it's a pleasant place to amble for an afternoon.

Octagon House Museum

Union and Gough streets ☎415/441-7512. Noon–3pm, second Sun, second and fourth Thurs of each month, closed January. Donation suggested. The work of Orson Fowler, a nine-

▲ OCTAGON HOUSE

teenth-century eccentric who published a book extolling the virtues of eight-sided living, was the inspiration for this oddball building in Cow Hollow. It's hard to miss, sitting defiantly in the middle of a small park, a neat blue-and-white relic of a long-forgotten fad (Fowler claimed eight-sided living was the answer to good health and long life). This particular octagonal home was built in 1861 by a local farmer, William McElroy, and the time capsule he stashed under the stairs was discovered during recent renovations; now on display, it offers a captivating glimpse at everyday life in early San Francisco, including letters, photographs, and a contemporary newspaper.

Palace of Fine Arts

Marina Boulevard and Baker Street ⓣ415/563-6504, ⓦwww.palaceoffinearts.org. Despite its name, this isn't a museum, but rather a huge, freely interpreted classical ruin that was first erected for the Panama Pacific International Exhibition held in the Marina in 1915. When all the other buildings from the temporary Exhibition were torn down, the palace was saved simply because locals thought it too beautiful to destroy. Unfortunately, since it was built of wood, plaster, and burlap, the palace gradually crumbled until the late 1950s, when a wealthy resident put up money for the structure to be recast in reinforced concrete. To the modern eye, it's a moody and mournfully sentimental piece of Victoriana, complete with weeping figures on the colonnade representing the melancholy of life without art. (The originals are now in the Exploratorium nearby.)

Exploratorium

3601 Lyon St at Baker. Information ⓣ415/563-7337, Tactile Dome reservations ⓣ415/561-0362, ⓦwww.exploratorium.edu. June–Aug Tues, Thurs–Sun 10am–6pm, Wed 10am–9pm; Sept–May Tues, Thurs–Sun 10am–5pm, Wed 10am–9pm. $10, free first Wed of the month. Hands down the best kid-centric attraction in the city, this museum crams more than 650 hands-on exhibits into a small warehouse space, each of which helps explain the principles of electricity or sound waves or similar. It's renowned for the "Tactile Dome," a total sensory deprivation dome, explored on hands and knees – and not for the claustrophobic (reservations essential).

Presidio

It's little wonder that this vast wilderness park, which stretches across almost 1500 acres, is so craggy and unspoiled – it started out as a military base. Now open to all, the **Presidio** is a more rural alternative for a bike ride or hike than the manicured

▲ PALACE OF FINE ARTS

lawns of Golden Gate Park; stroll or cycle along part of the Pacific Coast Trail here for the not-to-be-missed views across the Bay and back to the skyline. The park's main entrance for drivers, cyclists, or pedestrians is from Lombard Street; the huge gate there leads to the main quadrangle of buildings that once functioned as a military headquarters and are now home to the Presidio Museum, Building 102, on Lincoln Boulevard and Funston Avenue (Wed–Sun noon–4pm, free, ⓣ415/561-4331). It showcases so-so military memorabilia alongside fascinating maps showing which parts of the city were worst affected by the 1906 earthquake and fire.

Golden Gate Bridge

As much an architectural as an engineering feat, the **Golden Gate Bridge** took just over four years to build and opened to traffic in 1937. It was the world's first massive suspension bridge, with a span of 4200 feet, and was designed to withstand winds of up to 100 miles an hour and to swing as much as 27 feet. Its ruddy color (known as International Orange) was originally intended as a temporary undercoat before the gray topcoat was applied, but locals liked it so much, the bridge has stayed orange ever since – and it takes more than 5000 gallons of paint annually to keep it that way. You can either drive, bike, or walk across: the toll for southbound cars is $3, although biking is more thrilling as you teeter along under the bridge's towers. It takes about half an hour to walk the bridge's span, but it's an awe-inspiring amble, what with the unbeatable views of the city and the craggy landscape of the Marin Headlands.

Shops

Bulo

3040 Fillmore St at Filbert ⓣ415/614-9959. This store sells quirky European shoes, with an earthy, retro feel. They're more functional than high fashion – think funky flats that'll easily handle the hills.

Girlfriends

1824 Union St at Laguna ⓣ415/673-9544. Cutesy women's clothing, sleepwear, and toiletries, all bearing the store's signature laundry line logo.

The Great Overland Bookstore Company

2848 Webster St at Union ⓣ415/351-1538. Cluttered with piles of books, this is a first-rate, old-fashioned store, featuring mint-condition first editions as well as cheap paperbacks.

Mikado Japan Center

1737 Post St ⓣ415/922-9450. Enormous Japanese record emporium where the staff will let you watch DVDs or listen to a catchy CD by the latest Japanese pop star before you decide to buy.

PlumpJack Wines

3201 Fillmore St at Greenwich ⓣ415/346-9870, ⓦwww.plumpjack.com. If you're looking for an obscure Californian vintage or just a reliable local staple, this place has an enormous, exhaustive selection of in-state wines.

Cafés

Bay Bread Boulangerie

2325 Pine St at Fillmore ⓣ415/440-0356. Gourmet bakery selling fruit-dotted breakfast breads and tasty, chewy macaroons.

Patisserie Delanghe

1890 Fillmore St at Bush ⓣ415/923-0711. Artisanal French bakery, run by two expats, who make flaky, buttery croissants and glistening fruit tarts for $2 or so – try the fruit brioche. There are a few tables in the window if you want to sit and eat.

Perry's

1661 Fillmore St at Geary ⓣ415/931-5260. Unhurried, offbeat Japantown café, serving delicious Coney Island hot dogs as well as dozens of flavors of ice cream.

Pizza Orgasmica

3157 Fillmore St at Greenwich ⓣ415/931-5300, ⓦwww.pizzaorgasmica.com. Cheapie pizza joint that's a delicious lunchtime pit-stop, serving gourmet pizzas available by the slice. There are a few tables if you want to linger; settle in for a while if you want to enjoy the $7.50 All You Can Eat daily special (11am–4pm).

Sapporo-ya

1581 Webster St at Post ⓣ415/563-7400. Bustling and basic restaurant that offers delicious, low-cost, home-made buckwheat ramen – made by the old-fashioned noodle machine on display in the window – served up in thick, flavorful miso or pork broths.

Zao Noodle Bar

2031 Chestnut St at Fillmore ⓣ415/928-3088, ⓦwww.zaonoodle.com. Sleek, modernist noodle shop in the Marina, with eat-in and take-out service: standard noodle dishes start around $9 – try the spicy edamame.

Restaurants

Ace Wasabi Rock 'n' Roll Sushi

3339 Steiner St at Lombard ⓣ415/567-4903. Fast, cheap, and loud, dishing up a touch of rock 'n' roll attitude with every order; stop by at 6pm week-

▼ A VIEW FROM PACIFIC HEIGHTS

nights to play bingo – the winner gets $20 off their bill. Ask for the delicious, off-menu dragon egg roll (spicy tuna, wrapped in avocado).

Baker Street Bistro

2953 Baker St at Lombard ⓣ415/931-1475, ⓦwww.bakerstbistro.citysearch.com. Cramped but charming French café with a few outdoor tables where the $14.50 prix fixe dinner is a bargain – it's usually soup and dessert plus a simple lamb chop or pork belly. It's hard to find, nestled on a Cow Hollow side street in the shadow of the Presidio.

Bistro Yoffi

2231 Chestnut St at Pierce ⓣ415/885-5133. Charming mid-price Marina bistro, packed with potted ferns and mismatched chairs, and serving eclectic modern American dishes. The chef's especially known for her skill with desserts – try the vanilla bean crème brulée.

Café Kati

1963 Sutter St at Fillmore ⓣ415/775-7313, ⓦwww.cafekati.com. Small and eclectic restaurant with an outdoor patio, known for its adventurous fusion of Asian, Californian, and French cooking. The menu's a gourmet, if expensive, treat, featuring dishes like masala-rubbed salmon; expect to pay at least $20 per entree.

Ella's

500 Presidio Ave at California ⓣ415/441-5669, ⓦwww.ellassanfrancisco.com. The most notorious breakfast wait in town, so put on some comfortable shoes. It's worth hanging around, though, for the food, mostly Californian interpretations of American classics like mandarin pancakes with mango syrup.

Greens

Fort Mason Center, Building A ⓣ415/771-6222, ⓦwww.greensrest.citysearch.com. This is the queen of San Francisco's vegetarian restaurants. Upsides include its picturesque setting on a pier and adventurous dishes, like filo pastry layered with artichokes; downsides are the surly service and the unusually high prices for vegetarian dishes ($16–19 per entree).

Habana

2080 Van Ness Ave at Pacific ⓣ415/441-CUBA, ⓦwww.habana1948.com. Upscale and lively Cuban eatery, serving modern twists on staples, including *ropa nueva*, where a juicy chunk of steak sits on top of a traditional shredded beef stew. Entrees run $16–19.

▼ SUSHI AT JAPAN CENTER

Maki

1825 Post St at Webster ⓣ415/921-5125. Japan Center restaurant specializing in *wappan meshi* – a wood steamer filled with vegetables, meat, and rice – but popular as much

▲ A VIEW FROM THE PRESIDIO

for its warm, friendly owner as the food.

On the Bridge

1581 Webster St at Post ⓣ415/922-7765. Smallish Japan Center cafeteria serving *yoshoko*, or westernized Japanese food, such as spaghetti with *kim chi* (pickled cabbage) for around $5 a dish.

Sociale

3665 Sacramento St at Locust ⓣ415/921-3200. Intimate Italian bistro, nestled in a small courtyard at the end of a tiny alleyway, that's worth seeking out for its mostly light, Cal-Italian menu that features herby veal steaks and light pastas. There's barely room for 30 people, so come early or expect a wait. Entrees hover around $18.

Bars

City Tavern

3200 Fillmore St at Greenwich ⓣ415/567-0918. The best of the yuppie haunts that dot the Marina, this bar attracts a youngish crowd of preppy, clean-cut professionals. It's the favored place to sip a Chardonnay in a chic meat-market setting.

Perry's

1944 Union St at Buchanan ⓣ415/922-9022. Made legendary by Armistead Maupin's *Tales of the City*, this lowlit Cow Hollow institution is a hugely popular pub and a friendly place to grab a pint.

Clubs and live music

Boom Boom Room

1601 Fillmore St at Geary ⓣ415/673-8000, ⓦwww.boomboomblues.com. Gritty venue near Japan Center that was owned by the late bluesman John Lee Hooker until his death in 2001 and plays host to a fine selection of touring blues and funk artists. Cover $5–12.

The Fillmore Auditorium

1805 Geary St at Fillmore ⓣ415/346-6000, ⓦwww.thefillmore.com. The Fillmore was at the heart of the 1960s counterculture and reopened in 1994 after several years' hiatus; it's home now to rock and alt-rock touring acts. Cover varies.

`SoMa

SoMa (the area SOuth of MArket) had been an industrial wasteland from the city's earliest days but took an unimaginable upswing in the mid-1990s, thanks to Internet start-up companies that flocked to the district and its rockbottom rents. SoMa's revival crashed alongside the dot-com dream in early 2000, forcing many restaurants and bars to close, but the area's slowly regaining its spark, especially thanks to a slew of hot nightclubs. Note that despite the recent boom, there are still parts of SoMa that are downright dangerous even during the day – most notably Sixth Street – so stay accordingly alert and keep valuables hidden.

Palace Hotel

Originally built in 1875, this palatial hotel (hence the name) at Market and Montgomery (see p.168) was a symbol of San Francisco's swaggering new wealth. It burnt down during the 1906 fire, but was lavishly reconstructed – and though subsequent renovations have dampened most of its glories, the Garden Court dining room, where you can enjoy high tea today, still boasts its original 1875 Austrian crystal chandeliers suspended from a ceiling made from 72,000 panes of glass.

Cartoon Art Museum

655 Mission St at New Montgomery ⓣ415/227-8669, ⓦwww.cartoonart.org; Tues–Sun 11am–5pm; $6. Housed in a massive slab concrete gallery space, this inventive museum curates rotating exhibits of cells and drawings, usually a sprightly mix of high-concept "art-oons" by the likes of French illustrator Moebius as well as staples like Peanuts.

▼ GARDEN COURT AT PALACE HOTEL

Yerba Buena Gardens

Mission and 3rd streets ⓦwww.yerbabuenagardens.com; Daily sunrise–10pm; free. An iconic example of urban reclamation, these gardens are a rare instance of successful greenspace development. Not only has the park been seamlessly integrated into the surrounding area, but the inviting lawns and benches are often packed with picnicking office workers on warm weekday lunchtimes. Stretching along the park's eastern face is a magnificent fifty-foot granite waterfall memorial to Martin Luther King, Jr, inscribed with extracts from his speeches; while on the terrace above lies a Sister Cities garden, featuring flora from each of the thirteen cities worldwide that is twinned with San Francisco.

San Francisco Museum of Modern Art

151 3rd St at Mission ⓣ415/357-4000, ⓦwww.sfmoma.org; Fri–Tues 11am–

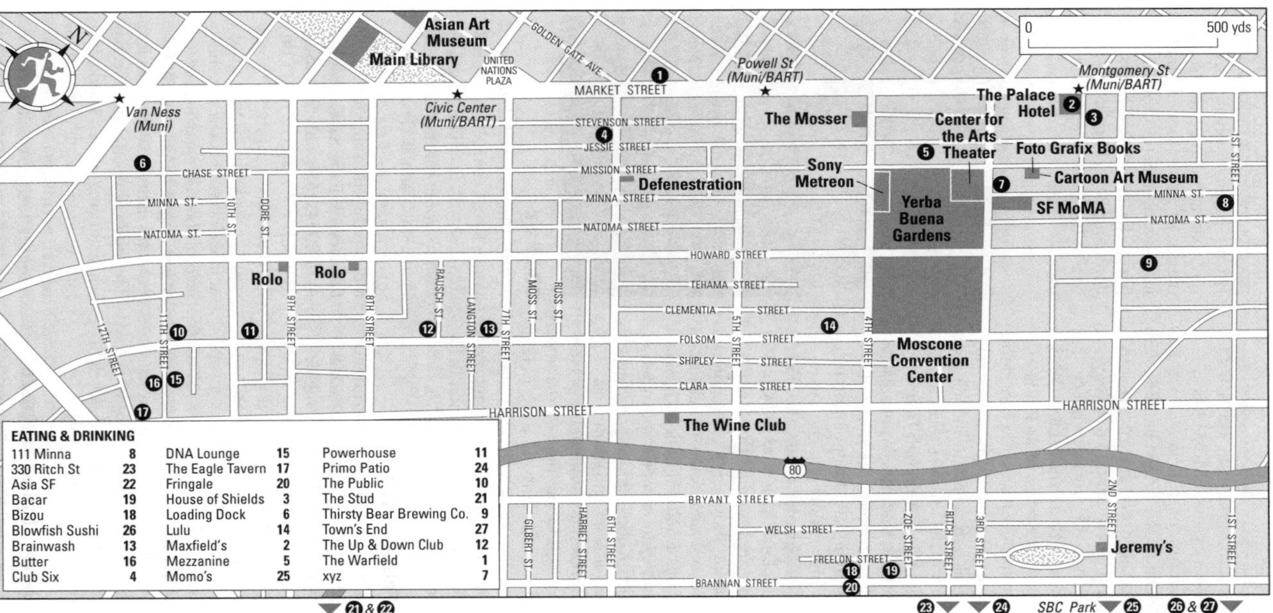
0
500 yds
Asian Art Museum
Main Library
UNITED NATIONS PLAZA
GOLDEN GATE AVE.
Powell St (Muni/BART)
Montgomery St (Muni/BART)
Van Ness (Muni)
Civic Center (Muni/BART)
MARKET STREET
The Palace Hotel
The Mosser
Center for the Arts Theater
Foto Grafix Books
Cartoon Art Museum
SF MoMA
Sony Metreon
Yerba Buena Gardens
Moscone Convention Center
Defenestration
Rolo
Rolo
The Wine Club
Jeremy's
SBC Park
STEVENSON STREET
JESSIE STREET
MISSION STREET
MINNA STREET
NATOMA STREET
CHASE STREET
MINNA ST.
NATOMA ST.
10TH ST.
DORE ST.
HOWARD STREET
TEHAMA STREET
CLEMENTIA STREET
FOLSOM STREET
SHIPLEY STREET
CLARA STREET
HARRISON STREET
BRYANT STREET
WELSH STREET
FREELON STREET
BRANNAN STREET
12TH STREET
11TH STREET
9TH STREET
8TH STREET
RAUSCH ST.
LANGTON STREET
7TH STREET
MOSS ST.
RUSS ST.
5TH STREET
4TH STREET
GILBERT ST.
HARRIET STREET
6TH STREET
ZOE STREET
RITCH STREET
3RD STREET
2ND STREET
1ST STREET
80
21 & 22
23
24
25
26 & 27
EATING & DRINKING
111 Minna 8
330 Ritch St 23
Asia SF 22
Bacar 19
Bizou 18
Blowfish Sushi 26
Brainwash 13
Butter 16
Club Six 4
DNA Lounge 15
The Eagle Tavern 17
Fringale 20
House of Shields 3
Loading Dock 6
Lulu 14
Maxfield's 2
Mezzanine 5
Momo's 25
Powerhouse 11
Primo Patio 24
The Public 10
The Stud 21
Thirsty Bear Brewing Co. 9
Town's End 27
The Up & Down Club 12
The Warfield 1
xyz 7

6pm, Thurs 11am–9pm, closed Wed; $10, $5 Thurs 6–9pm, free the first Tues of the month. SFMOMA is as famous for its premises as its collection; the striped building with its sliced-off center turret, looking like an albino boiled egg, was designed by Swiss architect Mario Botta and built in 1995 at a reported cost of $62 million. Inside, the turret's skylight floods the space with light while you walk across vertigo-inducing slatted metal catwalks that connect the floors. Although Botta's bizarre landmark is undeniably showstopping, the museum's holdings are disappointing in comparison: highlights are its photographic print collection (look for Man Ray and Cartier-Bresson, among others) plus a strong showing of cult California School favorites like Diebenkorn, Frida Kahlo, and Diego Rivera and some snappy Pop Art pieces (Jeff Koons's gilded porcelain statue of Michael Jackson and Bubbles, for example). It's better to spend more time on the upper floors checking out the traveling exhibitions, which often supply the arty spark that's missing from the museum's own earnest holdings.

Folsom Street

Though windswept and nondescript by day, this street fizzes with bars and clubs at night, especially those catering to the city's leather fetishists: if chaps and public whippings are your bag, make sure to book a trip back in late September for the **Folsom Street Fair** (between Eighth and Eleventh streets ⓣ415/861-3247, ⓦwww.folsomstreetfair.com), a celebration of all things fetish.

Defenestration sculpture

214 6th St at Mission. A quixotic piece of public art by local artist Brian Goggin, involving furniture that has been bolted to the outside of an abandoned building – worth a detour for a quick photo during daylight hours, but don't linger too long as this is one of the nastier corners in town.

▼ FOLSOM STREET BAR AT NIGHT

SBC Park

24 Willie Mays Plaza at 3rd and King streets ⓣ415/972-1800, ⓦwww.sfgiants.com. The new, $357 million home for the San Francisco Giants is clearly an improvement over the team's old, windswept home at Candlestick Park. **SBC** (Pac Bell until 2004) took only 28 months to build, and made its debut on the opening day of the 2000 season. The stadium, in one of the sunniest parts of town, has the second shortest right field in major league baseball (at 309 feet, only Fenway Park bests it). The outfield opens onto the Bay, where, during games, kayakers lurk, waiting to catch home runs. In fact, permission was required from the League to allow the design and many grumble that it

was specifically intended to allow star **Barry Bonds** to hit home runs more easily. He's the anchor of the team, an All Star outfielder, who shattered the season home run record (he hit 73 out of the park) and, in 2002, led the Giants to their first World Series since the 1980s.

The season runs April–September, and **tickets** are a hot commodity – though 500 bleacher seats go on sale four hours in advance on every game day (check the website for schedules, prices, and availability). If you can't snag a seat or are visiting in the wintertime, you can still see the inside of the stadium, walk on the field, and sit in the comfy padded dugout seats, thanks to the superb tours that leave from the dugout store on Third Street (daily except on home game days, 10.30am & 12.30pm, $10).

Shops

Jeremy's

2 South Park at 2nd ⓣ415/882-4929. Consignment and secondhand store specializing in casual and designer clothes for men and women, seconds, and fashion show outtakes.

▼ WILLIE MAYS STATUE AT SBC PARK

Rainbow Grocery

1745 Folsom St at 13th ⓣ415/863-0620, ⓦwww.rainbowgrocery.coop. Progressive politics and organic food in this huge wholefood store.

Rolo

1235 Howard St at 8th ⓣ415/355-1122, ⓦwww.rolo.com; 1301 Howard St at 9th ⓣ415/861-1999. Funky, unisex retailer with one of the best, most browsable selections of casualwear in town: 1235 Howard stocks denim and streetwear (Energie, Earl) while 1301 Howard is for end-of-line reductions and skate punk fashions.

The Wine Club

953 Harrison St at 6th ⓣ415/512-9086, ⓦwww.thewineclub.com. Huge warehouse space where the wine is offered at budget prices in torn cardboard boxes on the floor – tastings on Saturday afternoons.

Cafés

Brainwash

1122 Folsom St at 7th ⓣ415/861-FOOD. Gimmicky but fun: burgers, salads, or sandwiches are available while your laundry spins at the attached laundromat.

Primo Patio

214 Townsend at 3rd ⓣ415/957-1129. There's a massive covered patio hidden out back, dotted with mismatched umbrellas and old furniture. They serve sandwiches and burgers with a Brazilian or Caribbean twist, like jerk chicken or the Belize burrito, for around $6–7.

Town's End

2 Townsend St at Embarcadero ⓣ415/512-0749. Gourmet brunch spot,

famed for its tasty basket of baked goods that's served instead of bread. The food's modern American (smoked chicken hash and the like) and most entrees cost $9.50–11.

Restaurants

Bizou

598 4th St at Brannan ⓣ415/543-2222. French-Cal bistro with warm Mediterranean decor and service that's good for such a relaxed place. Try the delicate braised beef cheeks, followed by a sumptuous vanilla sundae.

Blowfish Sushi

2170 Bryant St at York ⓣ415/285-3848. Funky Asian fusion food, served to a thumping dance music soundtrack and with huge screens playing *anime* movies above the sushi bar. Try the ritsuroll, a tempura-battered combination of tuna, nori, and avocado.

Fringale

570 4th St at Brannan ⓣ415/543-0573, ⓦwww.fringale.citysearch.com. A romantic charmer, with service as exceptional as its food; the menu is predominantly French with a few Basque ingedients, like tangy serrano ham.

The frisee salad coated with egg and bacon dressing is delicious ($8), as are the buttery, rich, after-dinner truffles. It's expensive (entrees run $16–20, and wines are pricey) but worth every penny.

▼ F MUNI TROLLEY

Lulu

816 Folsom St at 4th ⓣ415/495-5775, ⓦwww.restaurantlulu.com. Yuppie foodie haven, offering family-style, Cal-Ital dishes in a rustic, rather cramped dining room: the pearl-sized gnocchi are meltingly fluffy. It isn't cheap, though, and some dishes can be hit and miss.

Momo's

760 2nd St at King ⓣ415/227-8660, ⓦwww.momos.com. Mainstream sports bar with a surprisingly swish and upscale attached restaurant where the food's clever and tasty (think fruity pork loin with dried cherry reduction). The bar's a meat market, especially after Giants home games.

The Public Restaurant and Bar

1489 Folsom St at 11th ⓣ415/552-3065, ⓦwww.thepublicsf.com. This newbie eatery is decked out in mismatched thrift-store decor and serves midprice modern American food. The two bars, thanks to live DJs and cheap happy hour martinis, make it a good choice for hip, heavy-drinking dates.

Thirsty Bear Brewing Company

661 Howard St at 2nd ⓣ415/974-0905, ⓦwww.thirstybear.com. Combination brew-pub and tapas bar: don't let the dull name put you off the delicious food, like fluffy potato *croquetas* and crunchy fried cala-

mari ($6–8 per plate). The sampler of in-house brews, featuring nine shot glasses each filled with a different blend ($4.50), is a delicious and cheap way to experiment.

xyz

inside the *W Hotel*, 181 3rd St at Howard ⓣ415/817-7836. Low-lit, sleek, and chic, this restaurant serves crisply prepared and well-presented dishes like fig wrapped in pancetta at expense-account prices.

Bars

111 Minna

111 Minna St at 2nd ⓣ415/974-1719, ⓦwww.111minnagallery.com. Stark, funky loft space that is a combination bar/art gallery/ performance space, usually with live DJs in the evening. The front room, with mismatched couches, is for chatting; it's more raucous in the rear by the tiny stage.

Asia SF

201 9th St at Howard ⓣ415/255-2742, ⓦwww.asiasf.com. Don't dare call them drag queens – the waitresses here are "gender illusionists" and perform campy burlesque on the bar throughout the evening. Try one of the delicious but deadly sake martinis.

Bacar Restaurant and Wine Salon

448 Brannan St at 4th ⓣ415/904-4100, ⓦwww.bacarsf.com. The loungey downstairs bar at this three-level restaurant is filled with overstuffed chairs where you can sample one of the hundred-plus wines served by the glass.

Butter

354 11th St at Folsom ⓣ415/863-5964, ⓦwww.smoothasbutter.com. Stylized "white trash" bar, featuring imitation trailerpark decor and serving junk food – its tag line is "Two turntables and a microwave." Fun, but not quite as hip as it once was.

The Eagle Tavern

398 12th St at Harrison ⓣ415/626-0880, ⓦwww.sfeagle.com. Gay leather bar most popular on Sundays when it holds a late-afternoon "beer bust" for charity.

House of Shields

39 New Montgomery St at Mission ⓣ415/495-5436. Old-school, clubby piano bar, opened in 1908, that's preserved its longterm decor (dark wood paneling) and long-term regulars (slightly crumpled businessmen).

Loading Dock

1525 Mission St at 11th ⓣ415/864-1525, ⓦwww.loadingdocksf.com. This gay bar is fetish heaven, with a strict dress code of leather, uniform, or denim as well as an on-site playroom.

Maxfield's

inside the *Palace Hotel*, 2 New Montgomery St at Market ⓣ415/392-8600. Mahogany-paneled, mural-decorated room that's a secluded and elegant place for a martini or two.

Powerhouse

1347 Folsom St at Doré Alley ⓣ415/861-1790. One of the city's prime pick-up joints, this gay bar has a strict dress code of uniform and leather – except on Thursday, which is underwear night.

Performing arts and film

The Center for the Arts

Theater
701 Mission St at 3rd ⓣ415/978-ARTS, ⓦwww.yerbabuenaarts.org. 750-seat theater hosting performances by prominent avant-garde dance, theater, and music companies. $10 and up

Sony Metreon
101 4th St at Mission ⓣ415/537-3400, ⓦwww.metreon.com. The only megaplex within walking distance of downtown, with fifteen screens of first-run movies.

Clubs and live music

330 Ritch St
330 Ritch St at Townsend ⓣ415/541-9574. The only constant at this small, out-of-the-way club is its location: different nights attract wildly varied crowds, but it's best known for the Thursday Britpop Popscene party. $5–15.

Club Six
60 6th St at Market ⓣ415/863-1221. Mixed gay-straight club, with a program that focuses on trance and hardcore dance music. On one of the nastier blocks in town, so be careful as you arrive and leave. $5.

DNA Lounge
375 11th St at Harrison ⓣ415/626-1409, ⓦwww.dnalounge.com. Downstairs is a large dancefloor, while the mezzanine is a comfy, sofa-packed lounge where you can chill. $15–20.

Mezzanine
444 Jessie St at 5th ⓣ415/820-9669, ⓦwww.mezzaninesf.com. Massive megaclub with mainstream, brand-name DJs – make a reservation for the VIP Ultra Lounge if you're feeling flush and flash. $15.

The Stud
399 Folsom St at 9th ⓣ415/252-7883, ⓦwww.studsf.com. Legendary mixed/gay club that's still as popular as ever, attracting a diverse, energetic, and uninhibited crowd. Check out the fabulously freaky drag queen cabaret at "Trannyshack" on Tues. $5–8.

The Up & Down Club
1151 Folsom St at 7th ⓣ415/626-2388, ⓦwww.sitiosf.com. A mix of live and DJ-spun danceable grooves – there's usually jazz downstairs at this club co-owned by supermodel Christy Turlington. $5.

The Warfield
982 Market St at 6th ⓣ415/775-7722, ⓦwww.thefillmore.com/warfield.asp. A beautiful, Art Deco music hall that was home to vaudeville headliners in the 1920s and is now the setting for concerts by top-name touring bands. It's a smallish, intimate auditorium, with a dancefloor on the first

▼ YERBA BUENA GARDENS

The Tenderloin and Civic Center

The Tenderloin has long been one of the shabbiest sections of town, overrun with flophouses and homeless vagrants. Local bureaucratic paralysis has continued to aggravate the problem, and the area's now rougher than ever – especially the stretch of Taylor Street around Turk and Eddy, where it's worth keeping your wits about you day or night. But waves of new Pakistani and South Asian immigrants are slowly improving the area, as well as establishing some excellent cheap eateries. Indeed, its budget eating and bar scenes are the big reasons to swing through here. Civic Center may at first seem a stark contrast to its grubby neighbor thanks to the grand Beaux Arts plaza, built after the 1906 disaster as architectural evidence of the city's fierce civic pride. But in fact, it's just the Tenderloin with better buildings, equally crammed with the homeless who camp out on the piazza.

Glide Memorial Church

330 Ellis St at Taylor ⓣ415/771-6300, ⓦwww.glide.org. Services Sun 9am & 11am. Part church, part social service provider for the local poor, Glide is best known for its rollicking Sunday services, powered by a roof-raising gospel choir (it's well worth stopping by, but be sure to arrive at least an hour in advance to be sure of admission). Otherwise, step inside to see the **AIDS Memorial Chapel**, whose altarpiece triptych was the last work Keith Haring completed before his death from the disease.

Polk Gulch

Polk Gulch (Polk Street between O'Farrell and California) is the congregating point for the city's transgender community and a hub for the flesh trade; it was also home to several famous gay bars (now mostly shuttered). The one local landmark is the Mitchell Brothers' **O'Farrell Theater** at O'Farrell and Polk streets, the strip emporium once run by the pioneering pashas of porn, Artie and Jim Mitchell. The brothers haven't been in charge for some years (Jim shot Artie in 1991), but it's still a throbbing hub for the local sex trade.

City Hall

Dr Carlton B. Goodlett Place at McAllister ⓣ415/554-4799, ⓦwww.ci.sf.ca.us/cityhall. Mon–Fri 8am–8pm, Sat–Sun

▼ O'FARRELL THEATER

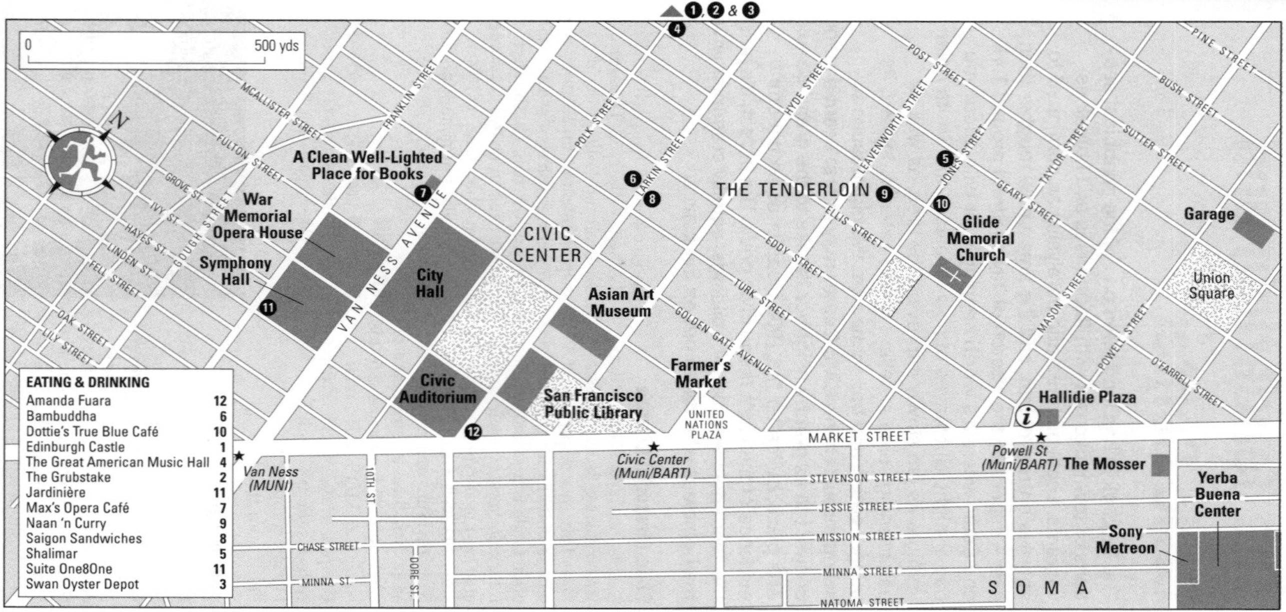

1, 2 & 3
4
0 500 yds
N

EATING & DRINKING	
Amanda Fuara	12
Bambuddha	6
Dottie's True Blue Café	10
Edinburgh Castle	1
The Great American Music Hall	4
The Grubstake	2
Jardinière	11
Max's Opera Café	7
Naan 'n Curry	9
Saigon Sandwiches	8
Shalimar	5
Suite One8One	11
Swan Oyster Depot	3

MCALLISTER STREET
FRANKLIN STREET
FULTON STREET
GROVE ST.
IVY ST.
HAYES ST.
LINDEN ST.
FELL STREET
OAK STREET
LILY STREET
GOUGH STREET
A Clean Well-Lighted Place for Books
War Memorial Opera House
Symphony Hall
VAN NESS AVENUE
City Hall
Civic Auditorium
CIVIC CENTER
POLK STREET
LARKIN STREET
Asian Art Museum
San Francisco Public Library
Farmer's Market
UNITED NATIONS PLAZA
HYDE STREET
GOLDEN GATE AVENUE
TURK STREET
EDDY STREET
ELLIS STREET
THE TENDERLOIN
LEAVENWORTH STREET
POST STREET
JONES STREET
GEARY STREET
TAYLOR STREET
Glide Memorial Church
MASON STREET
POWELL STREET
O'FARRELL STREET
SUTTER STREET
BUSH STREET
PINE STREET
Garage
Union Square
Hallidie Plaza
MARKET STREET
Van Ness (MUNI)
Civic Center (Muni/BART)
Powell St (Muni/BART)
The Mosser
Yerba Buena Center
Sony Metreon
10TH ST.
CHASE STREET
MINNA ST.
DORE ST.
STEVENSON STREET
JESSIE STREET
MISSION STREET
MINNA STREET
NATOMA STREET
S O M A

▲ CITY HALL

noon–4pm. Tours Mon–Fri 10am, noon, 2pm; Sat & Sun 12.30pm. Free. The current City Hall dates from just after the 1906 fire, when local architects Bakewell and Brown won the contest to design a new building, submitting a sketch inspired by the haughty, gilded dome of Les Invalides in Paris, where both had studied. Costing a staggering $3.5 million to build, City Hall is conspicuously sumptuous throughout, especially the astonishingly detailed, carved Manchurian oak walls in the Board of Supervisors Legislative Chamber. Recent earthquake retrofitting – which involved sliding giant ball bearings under its foundations – allows the entire structure to wobble more than two feet in either direction during an tremor. Although you can wander around the first floor of City Hall on your own, the best way to see the interior of the building is on one of the frequent free tours that even include a whistlestop walk through the mayor's private office.

San Francisco Public Library

100 Larkin St at Grove ⓣ415/557-4400, ⓦsfpl.lib.ca.us/. Mon & Sat 10am–6pm, Tues–Thurs 9am–8pm, Fri noon–6pm, Sun noon–5pm. Free. The sleek library building that opened in 1996 – replacing the older one, which became the Asian Art Museum – was controversial from the start because though it had a large, bright central atrium and plenty of space for lounging readers, there just wasn't that much space for books; many volumes were simply sold off. The big draw here is the exhibition space-cum-reference library known as the **James C. Hormel Gay and Lesbian Center**, the first of its kind in the nation. Otherwise, on the main floor, there are six Internet terminals that anyone can use free of charge for fifteen minutes, available on a first-come, first-served basis.

Asian Art Museum

200 Larkin St at Hyde ⓣ415/581-3500, ⓦwww.asianart.org. Tues–Wed & Fri–Sun 10am–5pm, Thurs 10am–9pm. $10, $5 after 5pm Thurs, free first Tues of every month. After the construction of the new public library, the

▼ SAN FRANCISCO PUBLIC LIBRARY

old library's home, built in 1917, was sensitively converted to house the **Asian Art Museum** by Gae Aulenti, the same woman who turned a derelict train station in Paris into the fabulous Musée d'Orsay. She swept away the dark bookstacks and opened up the interior to allow light to reach every corner, while still preserving details like the multicolored, ornamental ceiling decorations now visible in the upper galleries. The museum's holdings are vast, and it takes several hours to even hit just the highlights: the most famous treasure is probably the oldest known Chinese Buddha image, which dates back to 338 AD; there's also the wonderful wooden statue of Fudo Myoo, the wrathful Japanese god, with an expression more constipated than thunderous. Start browsing the holdings on the third floor and work down; there are free docent talks throughout the day, though it's better to skip the breathless, breakneck tours and stick with the audioguide. It's a shame the café's only accessible to paying visitors as it offers delicious Asian noodles and stir fries for $8 or so.

Shops

A Clean, Well-Lighted Place for Books

Opera Plaza, 601 Van Ness Ave at Golden Gate ⓣ415/441-6670. The stock at this local favorite is now more mainstream and less impressively exhaustive than it once was, but it's still worth checking out for the regular author readings – call for a schedule.

Heart of the City Farmer's Market

United Nations Plaza at Market St ⓣ415/558-9455. Wed & Sun 7am–5pm. A good place for a cheap picnic lunch, especially given the low prices – just double check the produce quality as it can be hit and miss.

Cafés

Ananda Fuara

1298 Market St at 9th ⓣ415/621-1994. Bargain vegetarian and vegan eatery with a vaguely cultish vibe: try the crunchy falafel or the impressive all-vegan mocha cake.

Dottie's True Blue Café

522 Jones St at O'Farrell ⓣ415/885-2767. Hefty portions of homemade cakes, eggs, and other breakfast favorites are the draw at this budget diner – plus its quirky owner Kurt who's always good for a gab. Breakfast and lunch only.

Saigon Sandwiches

560 Larkin St at Ellis ⓣ415/474-5698. Hole in the wall store selling made-to-order Vietnamese sandwiches for $2/each – the BBQ pork is a standout. Lunch only.

Swan Oyster Depot

1517 Polk St at California ⓣ415/673-1101. No frills at this cheap seafood counter in Polk Gulch, but it's beloved by locals for the fiercely fresh fish.

Restaurants

The Grubstake

1525 Pine St at Polk ⓣ415/673-8268. Daily until 4am. Old-fashioned diner, housed in a decommissioned cable car, that serves all the basics, though the specialty is "The Nugget," a bacon cheeseburger topped with a fried egg.

Jardinière

300 Grove St at Franklin ⓣ415/861-5555, ⓦwww.jardiniere.com. Indulge every culinary curiosity at this two-story rock-star restaurant – chef Traci des Jardins offers stunning, if pricey, French-Californian food (entree prices hover around $27–30) like gnocchi with oxtail sauce in the exposed brick, lowlit space. Make sure to get a table upstairs away from the bar where the setting's more intimate.

Max's Opera Café

601 Van Ness Ave at Golden Gate ⓣ415/771-7300. Surprisingly good value given its location on the plaza, this Jewish diner's known for philly cheesesteaks and matzo ball soup.

Naan 'n Curry

478 O'Farrell St at Jones ⓣ415/775-1349. Shockingly low-cost Indian restaurant in the Tenderloin that's rundown, but clean, and serves mouth-tingling curries for only $5.

Shalimar

532 Jones St at Geary ⓣ415/928-0333. Delicious, cheap Pakistani canteen-cum-café, where all the food is made to order before your eyes in the *kulcha* oven; there are a few tables on the sidewalk.

Bars

Bambuddha

inside the *Phoenix Hotel*, 601 Eddy St at Larkin ⓣ415/885-5088, ⓦwww.bambuddhalounge.com. Relaxed, groovy lounge, with a New Age-meets-Asian vibe (think swirling, elemental decor and *feng shui*-favorable fountains).

Edinburgh Castle

950 Geary St at Polk ⓣ415/885-4074. Just your average Scottish bar filled with heraldic Highland memorabilia – even though it's actually run by Koreans. The pub food's worth sampling, especially their impressive fish'n'chips. Upstairs is a venue that hosts comedy and rock acts.

Performing arts and film

San Francisco Ballet and San Francisco Opera

War Memorial Opera House, 301 Van Ness Ave at Grove ⓣ415/864-3330, ⓦwww.sfballet.org & ⓦwww.sfopera.org. The third oldest ballet company in the US (founded in 1933) remains in top form, thanks to artistic director Helgi Tomasson; while Iranian émigré Lotfi Mansouri

▼ NAAN 'N CURRY

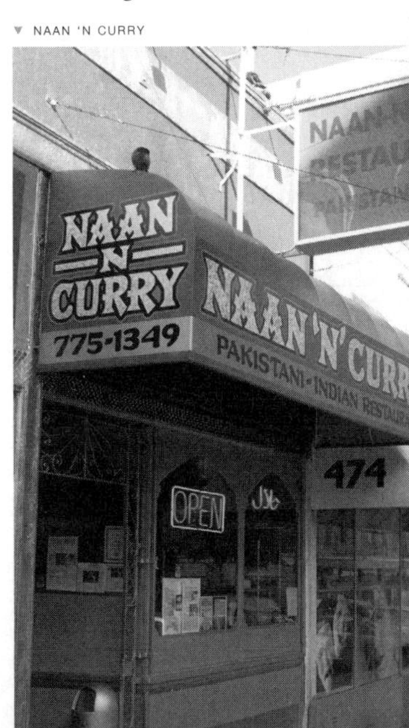

ensures a mix of avant garde operatic oddities alongside crowd-pleasing favorites. Ballet season runs Feb–May; opera season is Sept–Dec, with a short summer run June & July. Ballet tickets begin $30, while standing-room tickets for opera are only $15.

San Francisco Symphony

Louise M. Davies Symphony Hall, 201 Van Ness Ave at Hayes ⓣ415/864-6000, ⓦwww.sfsymphony.org. Once-musty institution that's been catapulted to the first rank of American orchestras thanks to publicity hound and premier conductor Michael Tilson Thomas. Season runs from September through May, with tickets starting at $25; $12 tickets for seats behind the stage are available two hours before performances.

Clubs and live music

The Great American Music Hall

859 O'Farrell St at Polk ⓣ415/885-0750, ⓦwww.musichallsf.com. Gorgeous, glamorous former bordello that plays host to a wide variety of rock, country, and world music acts. $10–20.

The Power Exchange

74 Otis St at Gough ⓣ415/487-9944, ⓦwww.powerexchange.com. Four-floor sexual playland, with themed rooms (leather, forest with tents, dancefloor) with both gay and straight areas. Cover varies.

Suite One8One

181 Eddy St at Taylor ⓣ415/345-9900, ⓦwww.suite181.com. High-end hipster bar-club, with live DJs, billowing white curtains, and a comfy king-size bed as a rest from the dancefloor. The heated outdoor patio's a major plus. $10 cover after 10pm.

The Mission

The Mission district remains one of San Francisco's unmissable delights, even if there are few official sights to take in (with the exception of the old church here, which gave the neighborhood its name). Long a center of San Francisco's largely working-class Hispanic community, in the past decade this area's also absorbed waves of artsy Anglos, closely followed by cool-hunting dot-commandos, who drove rents to once unthinkable heights. Even so, the district retains its Latin roots, both in the hundreds of murals splashed everywhere and via its profusion of authentic Central and South American eateries. Indeed, the nightlife and restaurant scene here is one of the most vibrant (and well-priced) in the city; keep in mind that the area does still have its sketchy corners, especially at night, and there can be gang activity on Mission Street between Fourteenth and Nineteenth streets.

Dolores Park

One of the best greenspaces in the city, this park is like a splash of fresh air in the neighborhood, otherwise so dominated by gritty urban streets. Naturally, Dolores Park is one of the best places to take advantage of the Mission's fog-free weather, with dozens of palm trees and rolling lawns spread over onto the side of a hill. The park's southwestern corner provides a spectacular view of the downtown skyline; on weekends, this chunk is known as Dolores Beach, as buff boys from the Castro come to bronze their gym-toned muscles.

Mission Dolores Basilica

3321 16th St at Dolores ⓣ415/621-8203, ⓦwww.graphicmode.com/missiondolores. Daily 9am–4pm. Free.
The city's oldest building, a squat, white adobe that has weathered both of the city's major earthquakes and was named after the day European settlers set up camp here (the Friday of Sorrows, before Palm Sunday), dates back to 1791. The first Mass celebrated on the site, in a now-destroyed shack thrown up in 1776, marked the official founding of San Francisco. The Mission's interior is hushed and simple, with a hand-carved eighteenth-century Mexican altarpiece and floor

▼ DOLORES PARK

plaques marking the burial sights of prominent locals. The attached woody, overgrown cemetery is home to the unmarked remains of more than 5000 Native Americans and also holds the remains of several notable San Franciscans – note how many names on gravestones match street names across the city. The showy, tiered wedding cake of a basilica next door

EATING & DRINKING

The Beauty Bar	20
Blondie's Bar & No Grill	15
Bombay Ice Creamery	14
Boogaloo's	24
Dalva	9
Destino	3
Doc's Clock	23
El Farolito	29
El Majahual	28
Emmy's Spaghetti Shack	30
Foreign Cinema	22
Hush Hush	4
La Cumbre	16
La Rondalla	21
Last Supper Club	27
Latin American Club	25
Liquid	11
Luna Park	18
Martuni's	1
Muddy Waters	13
Pauline's Pizza	5
The Phoenix	19
Radio Habana Social Club	26
Skylark	10
Sublounge	31
Tartine Bakery	17
Ti Couz	8
Waltzwerk	6
We Be Sushi	12
Wilde Oscars	7
Zeitgeist	2

▲ INTERIOR OF THE MISSION

was added in 1913 and holds little of historic interest.

Women's Building

3543 18th St at Guerrero ⓣ415/431-1180, ⓦwww.womensbuilding.org. Mon 9am–8pm, Tues–Thurs 9am–10pm, Fri 9am–8pm, Sat 10am–noon. Free. This community center hosts a variety of events and workshops, as well as a café, but is most notable for its exterior, tattooed with an enormous, sprawling mural known by the horrifically self-conscious name of *Maestrapeace*. On one side of the mural, there's an enormous mother-goddess figure, while on the other, a gigantic portrait of Rigoberta Menchú, the Guatemalan woman who won the Nobel Peace Prize in 1992.

Balmy Alley

There's barely an inch of wall in this small alleyway between Treat and Harrison streets that isn't covered in one of the Mission's famed murals; most are painted on wooden fences rather than stucco walls so they can be regularly replaced. Frankly, much of the artwork is more heartfelt than either skilled or beautiful, and the heavy-handed political imagery can be wearing; but the political themes do underscore how fiercely the Latin American heart of this neighborhood still thumps.

Valencia Street

This is the best place in the Mission to see how dynamically hip Anglo culture has fused with local Hispanic heritage – groovy boutiques and restaurants sit alongside age-old taquerias, and ambling down from 16th to 24th streets is a great way to spend an afternoon browsing and grazing.

Shops

Clothes Contact

473 Valencia St at 16th ⓣ415/621-3212. Secondhand clothing megaplex where you pay by the pound ($8), as weighed at checkout on a vintage scale – be prepared to rummage.

Dog Eared Books

900 Valencia St at 20th ⓣ415/282-1901, ⓦwww.dogearedbooks.com. Smallish corner bookstore with a snappy selection of budget-priced remainders, as well as an eclectic range of secondhand titles, all in terrific condition.

Good Vibrations

603 Valencia St at 17th ⓣ415/522-5460, ⓦwww.goodvibes.com.

▼ CEMETERY AT THE MISSION

Gloriously sexy co-op store designed to destigmatize sex shops. It's packed with every imaginable sex toy, plus racks of erotica and candy store-style jars of condoms.

HRM Boutique

924 Valencia St at 20th ⓣ415/642-0841, ⓦwww.hrmclothing.com. Best of the many one-off, local designer boutiques in the area, stocking smart, slightly retro menswear and kookier, offbeat women's clothing, most of it made on-site. Prices start at $50 for shirts.

Laku

1069 Valencia St at 22nd ⓣ415/695-1462, ⓦwww.lakuyaeko.com. Handmade exquisite silk slippers by local designer Yakeo Yamashita. Also sells velvet hair accessories.

Otsu

3253 16th St at Dolores ⓣ415/255-7900 or 1-866/HEY-OTSU, ⓦwww.veganmart.com. Closed Mon & Tues. Animal-free boutique, highlighting alternative materials including recycled tires and oilcloth for bags and belts, as well as a vast, impressive selection of shoes.

Subterranean Shoe Room

877 Valencia St at 20th ⓣ415/401-9504, ⓦwww.subshoeroom.com. Sneaker heaven with both this season's and classic styles from the likes of Nike, Asics, and Adidas – great for vegan athletes, too, since animal-free shoes are marked with a "V."

Cafés

Bombay Ice Creamery

552 Valencia St at 16th ⓣ415/431-1103. Tiny, authentic ice cream counter offers super-sweet, exotic flavors like cardamom and cashew-raisin.

Boogaloo's

3296 22nd St at Valencia ⓣ415/824-3211. Bright orange and yellow walls perk up this basic café, as does the hearty, Mex-inflected diner food; each dish costs around $5–7; make sure to order some chorizo (spicy sausage). Breakfast and lunch only.

El Farolito

2779 Mission St at 24th ⓣ415/824-7877. A scruffy, 24hr local institution, this formica-table-crammed taqueria serves terrific food, most especially the *quesadilla suiza*, with chicken and cheese.

El Majahual

1142 Valencia St at 23rd ⓣ415/821-7514. Salvadorean and Colombian eatery, marked out by its jaunty music and buzzing atmosphere, thanks to the local families who crowd in for dinner every night.

▼ EL FAROLITO

▲ VINTAGE CLOTHES SHOPPING ON VALENCIA

La Cumbre

515 Valencia St at 17th ☎415/863-8205. Old-fashioned taqueria with Wild West-inspired decor, staffed by chatty old women sharpening lethal carving knives before slicing meats to order. Burritos start at $4.95.

Muddy Waters

521 Valencia St at 17th ☎415/863-8006. A large café serving coffees, cakes, and pastries: it's a little careworn, but still the best neighborhood option for settling back with a book and a mug of coffee.

Pauline's Pizza

260 Valencia St at Brosnan ☎415/552-2050. Organic pizza joint that uses produce from its own garden for its delicious whole pies – the pesto pizza is a house special.

Tartine Bakery

600 Guerrero St at 18th ☎415/487-2600. Tasty croissants, creamy cappuccinos, and hearty crusty sandwiches at this gourmet bakery. There's no sign; just look for the green building.

Restaurants

Destino

1815 Market St at Guerrero ☎415/552-4451, Ⓦwww.destinosf.com. A small and welcoming restaurant, whose Peruvian chef-owner creates tasty, unexpected dishes like scallops in their shells coated in parmesan and juicy pork empanadas (large plates run around $17 or so). Wednesday's the night to come if you want to boogie, as there's tango dancing.

Emmy's Spaghetti Shack

18 Virginia St at Mission ☎415/206-2086. Unfussy, downhome eatery run by an artist, with a handwritten menu and chalkboard wine list. It's filled both with her handicrafts and with local hipsters who come for the cheap, tasty food like house meatballs for $8 or so.

Foreign Cinema

2534 Mission St at 21st ☎415/648-7600, Ⓦwww.foreigncinema.com. Upscale Cal-French restaurant where movies are projected onto the large outdoor wall while you eat – though the delicious food's attraction enough, especially the oyster bar at brunch. The industrial chic *Laszlo* martini bar next door, complete with DJ, is a place for after-dinner cocktails.

La Rondalla

901 Valencia St at 20th ☎415/647-7474. It's Christmas year-round at this Mexican dive, bedecked in tinsel and trinkets. The cheapish food's no better than average, but there's a handy take-out window and a full menu until 2am.

Last Supper Club

1199 Valencia St at 23rd ☎415/695-1199, Ⓦwww.lastsupperclubsf.com. Rustic and rowdy Italian restaurant, with gilt mirrors and distressed walls: don't miss the garlicky, parmesan-laced pesto that's served with the bread, or the gnocchi with shredded venison.

Luna Park

694 Valencia St at 18th ⓣ415/553-8584, ⓦwww.lunaparksf.com. Decked out like a lush bordello with deep red walls and ornamental chandeliers, this funky local favorite is always busy: the modern American entrees cost around $14. Save room for the tableside 'smores and one of the tasty cocktails like a Granny Smith apple martini.

The Phoenix

811 Valencia St at 19th ⓣ415/695-1811, ⓦwww.phoenixirishbar.com. Irish bar/restaurant serving hefty portions of pasta as well as a few Celtic specialties. It's well priced and a welcome change for the neighborhood.

Radio Habana Social Club

1109 Valencia St at 22nd. No phone. Quirky Cuban hole-in-the-wall, with tables jammed together and walls covered with picture frames and knicknacks. The food's cheap and tasty, the crowd eclectic.

Ti Couz

3108 16th St at Valencia ⓣ415/252-7373. Friendly, hip crêperie that's remained for several years as one of the best restaurants around in this price range, serving pancakes for $6 or so.

Waltzwerk

381 Van Ness Ave at 15th ⓣ415/551-7181, ⓦwww.waltzwerk.com. Closed Mon. An East German eatery offering thumping, hearty comfort food like pork schnitzel and sweet cabbage for around $10–14 per dish. The decor's speakeasy-inspired (red velvet sofas and the like) with framed East German pop records on the wall.

We Be Sushi

538 Valencia St at 16th ⓣ415/565-0749. Although grungy and a little inauthentic, this remains an unmissable, well-loved local institution. You can gorge on cheap sushi (most is $1/piece) while checking out what's on – the flyers on the walls are great for up-to-date neighborhood listings.

Bars

The Beauty Bar

2299 Mission St at 19th ⓣ415/285-0323, ⓦwww.beautybar.com. Campy, tongue-in-cheek bar outfitted like a 1950s hair salon – all bubblegum pink colors and retro dryers. You can even enjoy a manicure with your cocktail most nights.

Blondie's Bar & No Grill

540 Valencia St at 16th ⓣ415/864-2419, ⓦwww.blondiesbar.com. There's a wide selection of beers on tap at this local institution, which hosts a slightly older crowd and live music on its tiny stage. Smokers have their own cramped but handy room at the back.

Dalva

3121 16th St at Valencia ⓣ415/252-7740. Dark and divey wafer-thin

▼ RADIO HABANA

space that's popular with a diverse, artsy crowd and often squeezes live bands and DJs into the slender front room.

Doc's Clock

2575 Mission St at 21st ⓣ415/824-3627. Women-run alternative bar, with friendly staff and a spartan, Art Deco-style design – it's easy to spot thanks to the pink dayglo sign outside.

Latin American Club

3286 22nd St at Valencia ⓣ415/647-2732. Smallish bar with a pool table and walls covered in protest art; it's retained a neighborhood feel thanks to the reasonable prices.

Martuni's

4 Valencia St at Market ⓣ415/241-0205, ⓦwww.martunis.citysearch.com. Gay piano bar attracting a well-heeled, middle-aged crowd, all keen to sing along to classics from Judy, Liza, and Edith.

Sublounge

620 20th St at 3rd ⓣ415/552-3603, ⓦwww.sublounge.com. Futuristic jetset decor (airplane seats and video games) make this new lounge one of the city's hotspots – not to mention the fact that it's smoker-friendly.

Wilde Oscars

1900 Folsom St at 15th ⓣ415/621-7145. Gay pub decorated in an homage to the waggish wit, with quotations all over the walls; there's an Irish-inflected bar-food menu, too.

Zeitgeist

199 Valencia St at Duboce ⓣ415/255-7505. Grungy neighborhood biker bar, with 25 beers on tap and a patio where it often hosts BBQs.

Performing arts and film

The Roxie

3117 16th St at Valencia ⓣ415/863-1087, ⓦwww.roxie.com. Adventurous rep house and film distributor, often showcasing little-known documentaries or the work of first-time directors. Tickets are just $8.

Theater Artaud

450 Florida St at Mariposa ⓣ415/621-7797, ⓦwww.artaud.org. This converted warehouse space plays host to many of the best local dance and theater performers, and it's much less artsy than its pretentious name might imply. Tickets from $15.

Clubs and live music

Hush Hush

496 14th St at Guerrero ⓣ415/241-9944. Hidden bar/club with no sign that's nevertheless welcoming and friendly – whether you want to play pool or dance to retro cool music like nu disco or acid jazz with the slightly older crowd.

Liquid

2925 16th St at Capp ⓣ415/431-8889. Tiny, fun club with a mixed/gay clientele that's a rare place for serious dancing in the district. $5–10.

Skylark

3089 16th St at Valencia ⓣ415/621-9294, ⓦwww.skylarkbar.com. Yuppie-friendly hybrid club-bar, with low lighting and plenty of booths: there's a large dancefloor and DJ booth at the back. More bar on weekdays, more club at weekends.

The Castro

West of the Mission lies Eureka Valley or, as it's known around the world, the Castro. Claimed by San Francisco's gay community as it emerged as a group in the mid-1970s from the embers of Haight-Ashbury's hippie movement, the Castro quickly became synonymous with gay culture; it's one of the few places where straight people will find themselves in the minority. For such a lively and energetic area, there's oddly little here to see but rows of quaint houses and gay-friendly shops, but the out-and-proud vibe (not to mention some great restaurants) makes it a fun place to dawdle for an afternoon.

Harvey Milk Plaza

This plaza, on the corner of Castro and Market at the geographic heart of the city, was named in honor of San Francisco's first openly gay politician, who was murdered by Dan White, a jealous political rival, in 1978. In what became known as the "Twinkie defense," White claimed fast food additives had unbalanced his mind and so led him to shoot Milk; the judge clearly believed it since he only sentenced White to five years in jail. Today, Harvey Milk Plaza's a quiet place, home to a massive twenty-by-thirty-foot rainbow flag, the international symbol of gay pride that was first unfurled in San Francisco in the same year Milk died. Though it's sometimes used as a rallying point for protests, usually the plaza's oddly empty of people and acts mostly as a transit hub.

▼ PRIDE FLAG

Pink Triangle Park

Dedicated in 2002, this new monument (Ⓦwww.pinktrianglepark.org) is the first in the country to be dedicated specifically to the gay victims of the Holocaust; it's wedged into the sliver of land between Seventeenth and Market streets. There's a pink triangle at its heart, filled with rough rose quartz shingle; around this, amid dozens of spiky cacti, fifteen pink triangle-topped granite columns poke through. Each represents 1000 men who were murdered by the Nazis because of their sexuality.

Castro Theater

429 Castro St at Market Ⓣ415/621-6120, $8. This old-school movie palace was built in 1922 and is a stunning example of the Mediterranean Revival style, its exterior marked out by lavish stucco decoration and knobbly, ornate windows. Inside's equally opulent, with foamy balconies

and riotously over-the-top stucco ceilings. Also known as the **Castro Cathedral**, this movie palace often hosts campy revivals of 1940s classics, playing to the most enthusiastic audience in town. Be sure to arrive early for pre-screening performances on the "mighty" Wurlitzer organ; the musical medley always draws to a close with Judy Garland's hit *San Francisco*, with the crowd merrily clapping along.

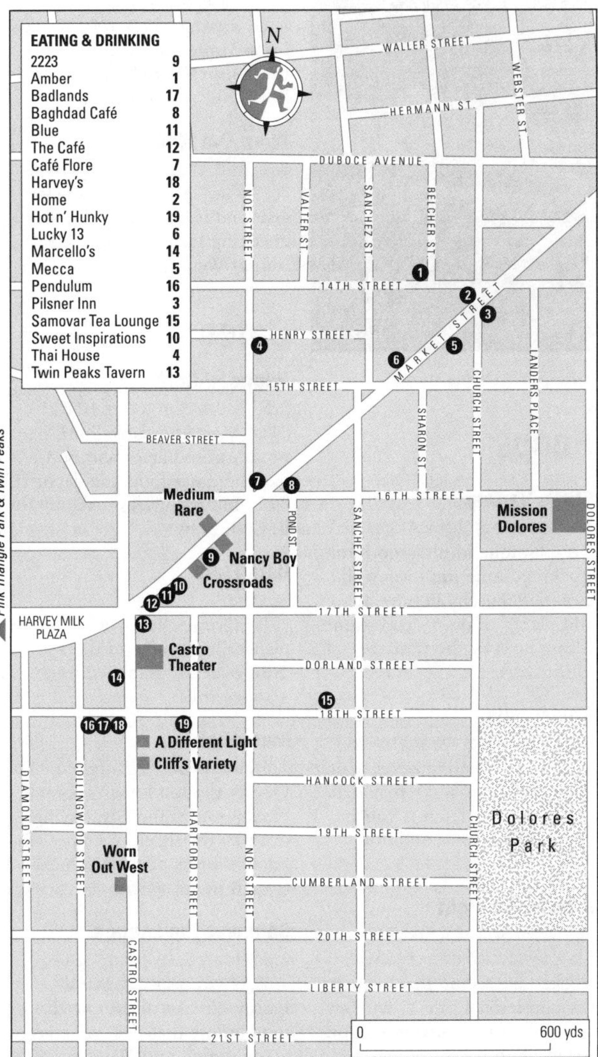

▲ CASTRO THEATER

Shops

Cliff's Variety

479 Castro St at 18th ☎415/431-5365. Unique local emporium, stocking home improvement essentials, kitschy homewares, and plenty of dress-up costumes (think boas by the yard). Unmissable.

Crossroads

2231 Market St at Noe ☎415/626-8989. Californian chainlet selling vintage clothes and remainders – it's not a steal, but is worth checking for top-condition basics.

A Different Light

489 Castro St at 18th ☎415/431-0891, Ⓦwww.adlbooks.com. Well-stocked bookshop that features gay and lesbian titles – with an especially strong fiction section – and often hosts readings.

Medium Rare

2310 Market St at Noe ☎415/255-7273. Tiny, diva-heavy music store crammed with hi-NRG and cocktail lounge classics from Donna Summer to Peggy Lee.

Nancy Boy

2319 Market St at Noe ☎415/626-5021, Ⓦwww.nancyboy.com. Kooky local cosmetics company, with the slogan "Tested on boyfriends, not on animals."

Worn Out West

582 Castro St at 19th ☎415/431-6020. Gay secondhand cowboy gear and leatherwear. Also worth checking for their wide selection of Western shirts.

Cafés

Baghdad Café

2295 Market St at 16th ☎415/621-4434. Most affordable 24hr option in the neighborhood – like the diner food, the decor is basic, but the prices make up for it. Cash only.

Café Flore

2298 Noe St at Market ☎415/621-8579. Cruisey café with a sunny, plant-filled courtyard that's a great place to grab a coffee and a gooey cake.

Marcello's

420 Castro St at 17th ☎415/863-3900. One of the top New York-style pizza joints in the city, serving pizza by the slice – it's especially known for its barbecue chicken-topped house special.

Samovar Tea Lounge

498 Sanchez St at 18th ☎415/626-4700, Ⓦwww.samovartea.com. Earthy, cushion-filled café that serves more than 100 varieties of tea as well as tasty Asian snacks –

▲ WELL-MAINTAINED VICTORIANS

the overstuffed wicker chairs are a great place to curl up with a book for the afternoon.

Sweet Inspirations

2239 Market St at Sanchez ⓣ415/621-8664. Tasty gourmet bakery with plenty of seating that serves dozens of different tarts and tortes – try a slice of the pear frangipane tart.

Restaurants

2223

2223 Market St at Noe ⓣ415/431-0692. This restaurant is one of the most mixed gay/straight venues in the neighborhood – likely both because of its friendly, chatty vibe and because everyone wants to sample the sumptuous, simple interpretations of California cuisine like lightly roasted chicken topped with onion rings. The setting's a soft, pale yellow room with high ceilings and low lighting; expect to pay $15 or so for an entree.

Blue

2337 Market St at Castro ⓣ415/863-2583. Smallish retro restaurant decked out in industrial chromes and blacks and serving deliciously simple comfort food, like chicken pot pie and chili, well into the early hours.

Home

2100 Market St at Church ⓣ415/503-0333. *Home*'s popular with a mixed crowd of guppies and yuppies, thanks to its groovy patio bar and DJ. The food's reasonable ($10–12 per entree) and mostly comfort staples like *moules frites*. Recommended.

Hot n' Hunky

4039 18th St at Castro ⓣ415/621-6365. This pink-and-chrome diner is a rather forlorn institution, with fading photographs of Marilyn Monroe on the walls, but the food's sprightlier than the atmosphere, with juicy burgers for around $4.

Mecca

2029 Market at 14th ⓣ415/621-7000, ⓦwww.sfmecca.com. Impressive, if expensive, nightspot that's first and foremost an impressive eatery that offers Californian cuisine with Asian inflections: the wood-fired pork tenderloin ($17.95) and seared tuna with parsnips ($23.95) are standouts. It's also a great place for a cocktail (the vodka mojitos are oddly delicious), especially on Weds when there's live jazz – if you're a fan, try to snag one of the dinner tables that overlooks the small performance area by the massive central bar.

Thai House

151 Noe St at Henry ⓣ415/863-0374. Warm, intimate neighborhood eatery that looks incongruously like a Swiss chalet: the corn

cakes are delicious, and the menu always offers quirky, tasty daily specials.

Bars

Amber

718 14th St at Market ⓣ415/626-7827. Mod bar, with retro mid-century fixtures, curtains made from dangling records, and old TVs. One of the few bars where smoking's permitted.

Badlands

4131 18th St at Castro ⓣ415/626-9320, ⓦwww.sfbadlands.com. Recently renovated video bar that attracts an attractive thirtysomething crowd. It's usually packed at weekends.

Harvey's

500 Castro St at 18th ⓣ415/431-4278. Lively corner hotspot drawing a friendly gay crowd (and even the occasional lesbian), named in honor of Harvey Milk.

Lucky 13

2140 Market St at Church ⓣ415/487-1313. A primarily hetero, divey rocker bar, with more than 35 beers on tap and a jukebox packed with Clash classics.

Pendulum

4146 18th St at Castro ⓣ415/863-4441. Famous as the one place in the Castro that's popular among the black gay community; it's a low-key place to hang out, with pool tables and pinball, plus a smoker-friendly patio accessible via a smallish entrance in the back hallway. Thurs is women's night.

Pilsner Inn

225 Church St at Market ⓣ415/621-7058. The best neighborhood gay bar in the Castro, filled with a diverse, slightly older crowd playing pool and darts; has a large, smoker-friendly patio out back.

Twin Peaks Tavern

401 Castro St at 17th ⓣ415/864-9470. Famous as the first gay bar in America to install transparent picture windows (rather than black them out) in 1972; now it's filled with middle-class, older white men here to chat rather than listen to loud music.

Clubs and live music

The Café

2367 Market St at Castro ⓣ415/861-3846. One of the few places in the area with a DJ every night; music's mostly hi-NRG and house, and the dancefloor's tiny so be prepared to jostle the lesbians and swishy men who fill it most evenings.

Haight-Ashbury and around

Haight-Ashbury lent its name to an entire era, giving the neighborhood a fame on which it has traded mercilessly ever since. Once a middle-class suburb with its own massive amusement park, the area hit hard times until the 1960s, when the students who had moved into the beautiful but battered Victorians were at the vanguard of the city's rebellious scene. Today it's theme-park boho, crammed with hippie-dippie souvenir shops. Best make your visit brief – unless you've a strong interest in tie-dyes and bongs – and continue on to the neighboring districts of Hayes Valley and the Lower Haight. You'll find much more interesting shopping, decent streetlife, and some lovely greenspaces as well.

Haight and Ashbury streets

It's surprising how unheralded this intersection, once the most famous street corner in the world, is today. The only sign of its importance is the regular stream of tourists lining up to be photographed next to the street sign in homage to the Grateful Dead, who were snapped standing here in the 1960s and guaranteed that the words Haight and Ashbury were synonymous with free love and hippie values. As if to ram home the fact that the area's gung-ho glory days are long gone, there's now a branch of khaki-loving

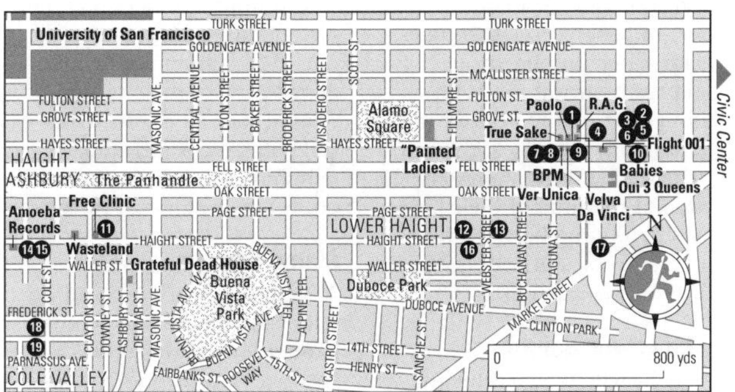

EATING AND DRINKING

Absinthe	6	Escape from New York	14	Mad Dog in the Fog	12	Stelline	3
Arlequin	5	Flippers	1	Marlena's	4	Suppenküche	7
Citizen Cake	2	Frjtz	8	Persian Aub Zam Zam	11	The Top	13
Crepes on Cole	18	Hayes and Vine	10	Powell's Place	9	Zuni	17
EOS	19	Kate's Kitchen	16	The Red Vic	15		

Hippies in the Haight

The hippie movement began in the 1960s as an offshoot of the Beats and stressed Eastern religion and philosophy as well as pacifism, but as it matured, drugs – notably LSD or acid, which wasn't illegal at the time – came to play a larger and larger role. The climax of this hippie revolution was 1967's Summer of Love, when more than 75,000 transitory residents called Haight-Ashbury home. Afterward, the mood in the Haight curdled, with heroin taking over as the drug of choice. It all burned out in the early 1970s, after which a splinter group of gay men – including hardcore hippie Harvey Milk – emerged, moved to the Castro, and founded the gay liberation movement.

corporate clothier the Gap on the corner.

▲ THE FAMOUS STREET CORNER

Grateful Dead House

710 Ashbury St at Waller. Much like the photogenic street sign on Haight Street, there's little to mark hippiedom's answer to Graceland, other than the clusters of people that sometimes gather here in pilgrimage. This old mansion was the band's home during the peak of its fame from 1965 to 1969, and where they were photographed around the time of their notorious 1967 drug bust. Be aware that it's now a private home, so stay on the sidewalk.

The Lower Haight

The heavily wooded hilltop greenspace known as Buena Vista Park marks the unofficial divide between Haight-Ashbury and the area known as Lower Haight, which stretches along the main drag through to Fillmore Street. It's reassuringly free of both tourists and tie-dye T-shirt shops; instead you'll find record stores catering to local DJs at the forefront of the Bay Area club scene as well as a smattering of welcoming, locals-dominated bars and cafés.

Hayes Street

This thoroughfare, from Steiner to Van Ness, serves as the center for Hayes Valley, a chic, funky shopping district east of the Haight. It's lined with shady trees and sidewalk cafés, not to mention some of the coolest galleries and homeware and clothing stores around. The surrounding streets comprise one of the more racially integrated parts of the city, with bargain soul food restaurants and coffeeshops providing a refreshing counterpoint to the growing trendiness of the place.

Alamo Square

A manicured park perched on a hilltop, Alamo Square is most famous for the cluster of restored Victorians known as the "**Painted Ladies**" which overlook it from the east, at Steiner Street between Hayes and Grove. Built in 1894 and restored eighty years later in modern shades of hunter green, cream, and baby blue, the houses are unusual in that, although Italianate in style, they have gables – for more on Victorians' architecture, see p.100. And even if you've forgotten your camera, it's still worth the steep climb up here for the brilliant views across the city.

Shops

Amoeba Records

1855 Haight St at Stanyan ⓣ415/831-1200, ⓦwww.amoebamusic.com. One of the largest used-music retailers in America, offering a massive warehouse space filled with new and used CDs at bargain prices. Their original, somewhat bigger, location is in Berkeley (see p.150).

Babies

235 Gough St at Hickory ⓣ415/701-7383, ⓦwww.babiessf.com. The best shop for the hip, high-end pet and its owner – with a wall of assorted collars and jars full of biscuits like a candy counter.

BPM

573 Hayes St at Laguna ⓣ415/487-8680. One of the top DJ record stores in the city, with the latest UK imports from top-name British DJs and masses of flyers for upcoming events.

Flight 001

525 Hayes St at Octavia ⓣ415/487-1001, ⓦwww.flight001.com. Sleek, futuristic travel store selling books, accessories, and dapper carry-on bags.

Oui, Three Queens

225 Gough St at Oak ⓣ415/621-6877. Tiny, cartoonish salon producing custom-blended cosmetics, including lipsticks, at reasonable prices. The baroque, bejeweled space is worth checking out even if you're not a makeup maven.

Paolo

524 Hayes St at Laguna ⓦwww.paoloshoes.com. Local designer Paolo Iantorno is a little-known gem. He produces a limited edition (20–25 pairs) of his own fashion-forward men's and women's shoe designs in Italy, then sells them from his two stores in San Francisco for around $200.

R.A.G.

541 Octavia St at Hayes ⓣ415/621-7718, ⓦwww.residentsapparel.com. Closed Tues. Innovative, mini-department store specializing in local designers under 30 – each

▼ BPM MUSIC STORE

rents rack space to showcase their ranges. Most are surprisingly affordable, and the plus is that you'll never bump into anyone else wearing the same outfit.

True Sake

560 Hayes St at Laguna ⓣ415/365-9555 or 1-800/949-3267, ⓦwww.truesake.com. A funky, all-sake store that sells more than 100 different varieties. Each bottle is color-coded to show whether it's a light, crisp blend or a heftier, aged sake much like port.

Velvet DaVinci

508 Hayes St at Octavia ⓣ415/626-7478. Sumptuous jewelry store-cum-gallery that stocks art pieces by more than fifty designers from ten countries.

▼ VINTAGE SHOPPING

Ver Unica

437b Hayes St at Gough ⓣ415/431-0688, ⓔfashion@ver-unica.com. Vintage shop selling high-grade secondhand clothing alongside a few brand-new retro-inspired pieces, mostly by local designers.

Wasteland

1660 Haight St at Belvedere ⓣ415/863-3150. Located in an old building that was once part of the amusement park that kickstarted Haight-Ashbury, this store provides a high-end vintage selection, sorted by style and color.

Cafés

Arlequin

384B Hayes St at Gough ⓣ415/626-1211. Chi-chi patisserie with a subtle French accent, serving delicate breakfast pastries as well as lunchtime sandwiches for around $7. Make sure to head through the main café to the huge, secluded, flower-filled garden out back.

Citizen Cake

399 Grove St at Franklin ⓣ415/861-2228, ⓦwww.citizencake.com. Stylish, pricey café-bakery with a soft jazz soundtrack serving delectable, delicate pastries – its brunch specials, like eggy French toast with dried cherries ($9), are unmissable.

Escape from New York

1737 Haight St at Shrader ⓣ415/668-5577. Low-key pizzeria decorated with old LPs that sells both whole pies and warmed-to-order slices with traditional toppings.

Flippers

482 Hayes St at Octavia ⓣ415/552-8880. Great-value brunches and gourmet hamburgers (try the teriyaki and pineapple) for around $6. There's ample outdoor seating.

Frjtz

579 Hayes St at Laguna ⓣ415/864-7654. Trendy, tiny *friterie*, serving cones of crunchy Belgian-style fries with dips like tabasco-chive ketchup or spicy yogurt peanut.

Restaurants

Crêpes on Cole

100 Carl St at Cole ☎415/664-1800. The crêpes here are filling, inventive, and enormous – and most cost only $6.95 or so. Even better, every serving comes piled high with home fries.

▼ TATTOOS AND PIERCING AVAILABLE

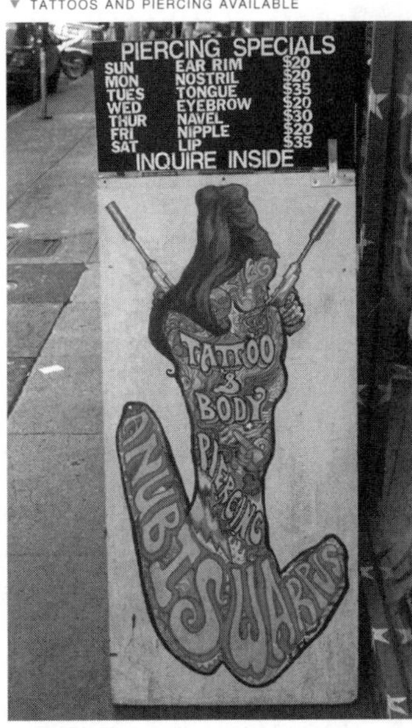

EOS

901 Cole St at Carl ☎415/566-3063. The spectacular East–West fusion food, like ginger Caesar salad or lemon grass risotto, is expensive but unmissable at this neighborhood favorite; there's a wine bar with a snack menu attached, if you don't want to splash out the money for a proper meal.

Kate's Kitchen

471 Haight St at Fillmore ☎415/626-3984. Monstrously huge portions of hearty breakfast food and crunchy hush puppies are the pluses at this small diner; the massive crowds at weekends are the minus.

Powell's Place

511 Hayes St at Octavia ☎415/863-1404. Southern fried chicken is the house specialty at this cheapie diner, but there are daily Southern specials like chicken fried steak. Every dinner is served with two sides as well, like grits or greens, as well as a couple of crumbly corn muffins.

Stelline

330 Gough St at Hayes ☎415/626-4292. Red-checkered tablecloths, a handwritten and photocopied menu, plus affable, chatty staff make this a standout among the cheap cafés nearby; entrees cost $6–7.

Suppenküche

601 Hayes St at Laguna ☎415/252-9289. There's a beerhall atmosphere at this German eatery, complete with bare walls and stark pine chairs and tables; entrees like Wiener schnitzel cost $12–17. Dinner only; Sunday brunch.

Zuni

1658 Market St at Gough ☎415/552-2522. Once nouveau and now a staple, *Zuni* features the most famous Caesar salad in town – made with home-cured anchovies – and an equally legendary focaccia hamburger made in a rustic Californian style; most entrees are in the $18–22 range. The minimalist, rather Nineties decor is heavy on brick and glass.

Bars

Absinthe

398 Hayes St at Gough ⓣ415/551-1590. The bar of this plush, velvet-draped brasserie-bistro is a handy option in the area, since it's open until 2am and serves smallish snacks for $6 or so per plate.

Hayes and Vine

377 Hayes St at Gough ⓣ415/626-5301. Fancy, dimly lit wine bar serving thirty different wines by the glass, many of them outstanding local varieties; the multi-glass "flights of wine" are usually well chosen.

Mad Dog in the Fog

530 Haight St at Fillmore ⓣ415/626-7279, ⓦmaddog.citysearch.com. Aptly named by the two British lads who own it, this bar offers darts, English beer, and copies of the *Sun* newspaper.

Marlena's

488 Hayes St at Octavia ⓣ415/864-6672. Old-school drag bar serving cheap drinks to a thirty- and fortysomething crowd of men and a few women.

Persian Aub Zam Zam

1663 Haight St at Clayton ⓣ415/861-2545. The retro jazz jukebox sets the tone at this Casbah-style cocktail lounge – the music's loungey and low key, as is the vibe. Once run by a notoriously finicky owner, his regulars clubbed together to buy the bar and preserve its old-fashioned ambiance.

Performing arts and filmFilms

The Red Vic

1727 Haight St at Cole ⓣ415/668-3994, ⓦwww.redvicmoviehouse.com. Grab a wooden bowl of popcorn and kick your feet up on the benches at this friendly cinematic collective where cult faves predominate.

Clubs and live music

The Top

424 Haight St at Webster ⓣ415/864-7386, ⓦwww.thetopdjbar.com. Tiny, dark DJ bar with a mixed gay/straight crowd that often hosts cutting-edge local turntablists. Cover $5–10.

▼ "PAINTED LADIES"

Golden Gate Park

Spreading three miles or so west from Haight-Ashbury, rolling, rustic Golden Gate Park is the lungs of the city; a visit here is essential to understand the outdoorsiness so central to the local character. Designed in 1871 by William Hall to mimic the style of Central Park-creator Frederick Law Olmsted, Golden Gate Park has more than a thousand acres of gardens and forest. The original plan was to keep the park free of buildings, but that proved impossible after the 1894 World's Fair was held here: the exhibition's legacy is the two major museums in the park's eastern end. From the outset, Golden Gate was to be a woodland park, and so the streets were artfully curved to encourage promenading. Today, it's hugely popular with locals for that very reason – they can jog through the park's paths or spend a summer afternoon picnicking here.

California Academy of Sciences / M.H. de Young Museum

Both of the park's museums were under reconstruction at time of writing. The original home for the California Academy of Sciences (ⓣ415/750-7145, ⓦwww.calacademy.org) is being gutted and reconstructed as a state-of-the-art facility that's scheduled to reopen in 2008. Meanwhile, the nearby M.H. de Young Museum (ⓣ415/863-3330, ⓦwww.thinker.org) is also closed so that its cramped, antiquated quarters could be leveled and replaced by a futuristic, copper-plated building with a geometric tower intended to blend with the surrounding plants as it develops a greenish patina with age. This project's close to completion, and the upgraded museum's scheduled for debut sometime in 2005. During renovations, you can still see some of the de Young's fine art collection by heading to its sister site, the California Palace of the Legion of Honor (see p.141).

Japanese Tea Garden

ⓣ415/751-1171. Daily 9am–6pm. $3.50. One of the best-known attractions in the park, this Asian fantasy of miniature trees and groomed plants was actually created for the 1894 Exposition by an Australian, George Turner Marsh, who had lived in Japan; and it was only once Marsh sold

Good fortune

The fortune cookie is certainly a California creation, but the arguments over whether it's Japanese or Chinese still rage. The most popular story of its invention involves Makota Hagiwara, the first Japanese owner of the Tea Garden. In 1907 (or so the story goes) Hagiwara was ousted from his job there by racist mayor James Phelan. Amid much protest, Hagiwara was quickly reinstated and invented the cookies as a way of delivering thank-you notes to those friends who'd championed his cause.

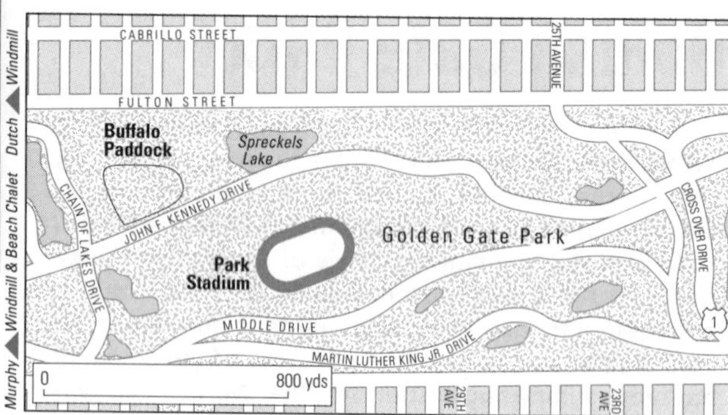

it soon after to the park's commissioners that a Japanese man took charge. A massive bronze Buddha cast in 1790 dominates the twisty, nook-crammed garden; make sure to climb the humpback bridge and check out the magnificent but careworn pagoda from San Francisco's Panama Pacific International Exhibition in 1915. The best time to enjoy the garden's tranquility is when it first opens, before the busloads of tourists start pouring in. If you're peckish and want to nibble on some cookies and sip a cup of tea, you'll need to fork over an additional $2.95.

▼ CONSERVATORY OF FLOWERS

Conservatory of Flowers

Ⓣ415/831-2700, Ⓦwww.conservatoryofflowers.org. $5. The redwood and glass building that houses the Conservatory of Flowers is a spectacular sight, supposedly modeled after the Palm House at London's Kew Gardens, though in fact it looks nothing like it. In fact, the building, with its whitewashed wooden frame, resembles the overblown greenhouse of a well-to-do Victorian country home. Its spiffy appearance hides a troubled history: it was closed in 1995 after severe storm damage rocked the building, necessitating the plants being shipped to local nurseries while the ailing conservatory was shored up. After eight years and $25 million worth of renovation and restoration, the conservatory finally reopened in Sept 2003. Now it's divided into five sections: a temporary exhibition space, a room filled with Victorian-style potted plants, lowland and highland tropics areas (in the latter, look for the spindly orchids from the Andes) and best of all, a cool, aquatic plant room that showcases its showstoppingly huge Victoria waterlilies.

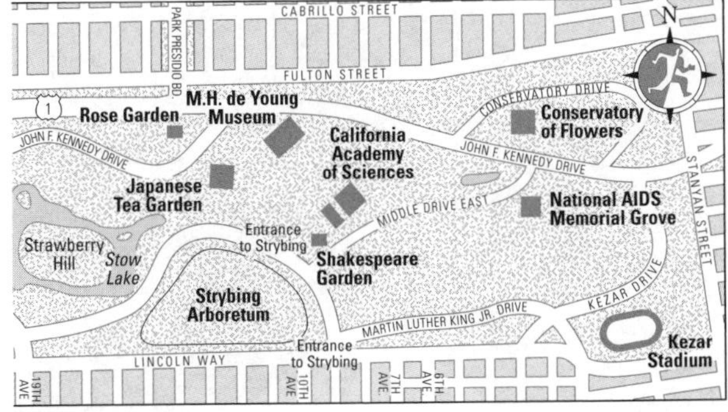

Strybing Arboretum

Ⓣ415/661-1316. Mon–Fri 8am–4.30pm, Sat–Sun 10am–5pm, tours Wed, Fri, Sun at 2pm. Free. This 75-acre botanic garden is home to more than 7000 varieties of plants, with its miniature gardens focusing on plants from different regions of the world – desert to tropical; especially appealing is the headily scented garden of fragrance. The main entrance is at Ninth Avenue and Lincoln Way on the park's southern edge.

AIDS Grove

Ⓣ415/750-8340, Ⓦwww.aidsmemorial.org. Set up in 1998, this seven-acre memorial garden was the first of its kind in the country, designed to commemorate those who died of AIDS-related illnesses as well as providing a serene place where loved ones could linger. Rocks with single names dot the edge of the large oval greenspace and, though a little rundown these days, it's still astonishingly peaceful.

Shakespeare Garden

This tiny, hedged garden, centered on an old-fashioned sundial and dotted with benches, showcases every flower and plant mentioned in Shakespeare's works, whether plays, sonnets, or poems. There's a metal plaque full of the relevant quotes on a brick wall at the edge of the lawn.

Buffalo Paddock

No one can say exactly why there's a small herd of bison in the park, but they're certainly a daunting and impressive sight – the best place to get close to them is in their feeding area at the far west end of the paddock.

The Windmills

Ⓦwww.goldengateparkwindmills.org. On the western edge of the park stand twin windmills. The

▼ DUTCH WINDMILL

▲ PAGODA IN THE JAPANESE TEA GARDEN

1902 **Dutch Windmill** to the north, which once pumped water to a reservoir in the park, was carefully restored to working order in the 1980s. To the south is the **Murphy Windmill**, which was built three years later and lags several years behind in restoration – for lack of funds, it's in a sorry state, but there's a local campaign to raise money enough to make it over.

The Beach Chalet

1000 Great Highway ⓣ415/386-8439, ⓦwww.beachchalet.com. This two-story, white-pillared building houses a series of 1930s frescoes depicting the growth of the city of San Francisco. Upstairs is the lively *Beach Chalet* brewery-restaurant that's a great place to grab a late weekend brunch; try the crab omelette and a pint of the Beach Blanket Blond Ale.

The Richmond and the Sunset

On the western edge of San Francisco, the fog-choked and forgotten districts of the Sunset and Richmond districts are on few visitors' itineraries – which is a pity, since there's plenty to see, including the California Palace of the Legion of Honor, which has a fair claim to being the best museum in the city. More than anything, though, both neighborhoods are refreshingly ordinary in comparison to the self-consciously visitor-friendly sites downtown. Today, the Richmond is often referred to as "new Chinatown," due to the Chinese residents who've thronged there in recent years, but it's also appealing for its enormous parks and handy beaches. The Sunset is more residential, with its swathes of identical post-war stucco houses, but nevertheless has quite a thriving niche of stores and restaurants huddled around the junction of Ninth Avenue and Irving Street.

Clement Street

This commercial drag is the hub of the thriving Chinese community that's flocked to the Richmond in recent years. Between Park Presidio and Arguello boulevards, the shopfronts are filled with dim sum stores, eat-in restaurants, and Chinese groceries, which makes for an atmospheric, authentically Asian way to spend a hungry afternoon – especially in comparison with the tourist-geared amenities in old Chinatown.

California Palace of the Legion of Honor

inside Lincoln Park ⓣ415/863-3330, ⓦwww.legionofhonor.org. Tues–Sun 9.30am–5pm. $8, $2 reduction with valid Muni transfer, free Tues. Built on a cliff-side hilltop in 1920 by Alma de Bretteville (see p.167) to resemble the Legion d'Honneur in Paris, this museum is an elegant Neoclassical building centered on a pillared courtyard. It houses Alma's staggering collection of works by the sensual French sculptor Rodin, which is more than reason enough to make the journey here. There are over eighty pieces, including bronzes, maquettes, and marble sculptures:

▼ CLEMENT STREET

standouts include *Fallen Angel, The Athlete,* and a small preparatory study for *The Kiss.* The Rodin holdings at this magnificent museum are somewhat let down by the other collections, including a lackluster set of Old Masters. Fortunately, the selection has recently been bolstered by the de Young's holdings, which were transferred here while it's being rebuilt. Bright spots of the combined holdings include some fine English portraiture from Raeburn and Gainsborough, plus lively Degas sketches and a small Seurat canvas. The basement space is used for a rotating display of touring shows that vary wildly in quality.

Lincoln Park & Land's End

The museum is surrounded by **Lincoln Park**, a craggy but beautiful greenspace carved into the coast at the northwestern-most tip of the city. There are several trails curving around the cliffs here that make for a pleasant hike, and it's worth trekking around to the section known as **Land's End**, one of the few true wilderness areas left in the city. Littering the base of its jagged cliffs are the broken hulls of ships that have failed to navigate the violent currents here; with luck, at low tide you can see chunks of the wooden wreckage. If you stay until dusk, there are spectacular views of

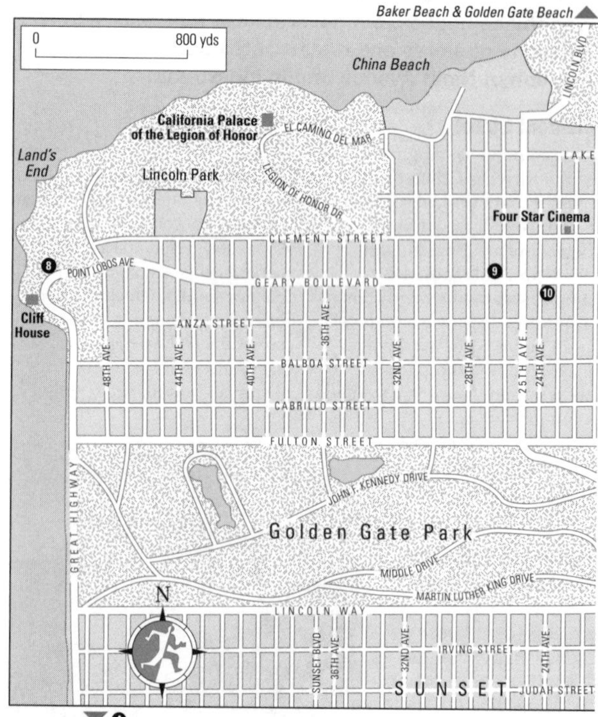

▲ LAND'S END

the Golden Gate Bridge and Marin headlands.

Baker, China, and Golden Gate beaches

Baker Beach is the most popular of the three, with wide, clean swathes of sand and easy access by Muni bus (#29) or car (there's ample street parking nearby). However, **China Beach** immediately to its south – reachable via a cluster of rocks at low tide – is more sheltered and has better facilities, including showers. **Golden Gate Beach** to the north is a predominantly gay and nude beach, and quite tricky to reach via a series of perilous trails; if you do make it, one

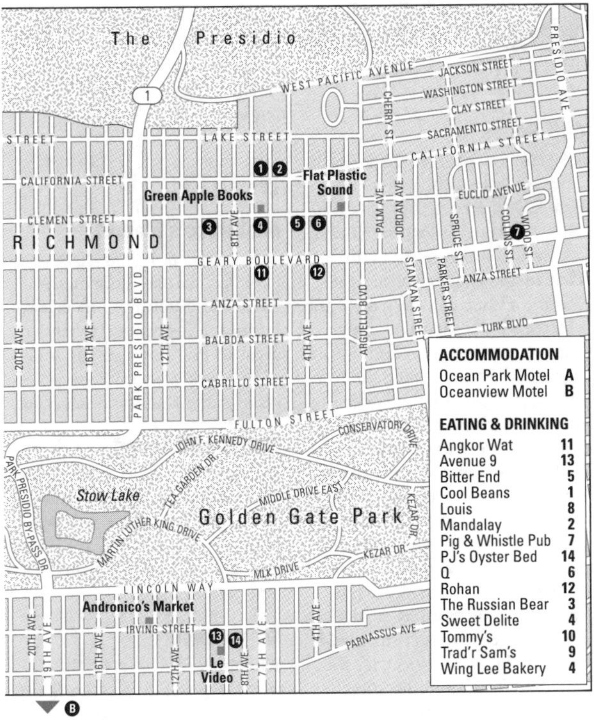

ACCOMMODATION

Ocean Park Motel	A
Oceanview Motel	B

EATING & DRINKING

Angkor Wat	11
Avenue 9	13
Bitter End	5
Cool Beans	1
Louis	8
Mandalay	2
Pig & Whistle Pub	7
PJ's Oyster Bed	14
Q	6
Rohan	12
The Russian Bear	3
Sweet Delite	4
Tommy's	10
Trad'r Sam's	9
Wing Lee Bakery	4

reward is a stunning view of the Golden Gate Bridge. Note that though all three beaches here may be inviting, the water is bone-chillingly cold and the currents fierce, so don't plan more than a quick paddle.

▲ RODIN AT THE PALACE OF THE LEGION OF HONOR

Cliff House

1090 Point Lobos Rd ⓣ415/386-3300, ⓦwww.cliffhouse.com. Mon–Thurs 9am–1.30am, Fri–Sun 8.30am–1.30am. Now simply a forlorn restaurant, it's hard to imagine that **Cliff House** and the area around it was the Fisherman's Wharf of the nineteenth century. The complex, containing rides and sideshows, was the brainchild of mining millionaire (and later mayor of San Francisco) Adolph Sutro and its centerpiece was Cliff House. The owners of the house's current, architecturally challenged incarnation (several previous versions burned down) are attempting to spiff it up via an exhaustive and lengthy renovation. Renovations aside, the reason to stop by isn't the bland, modern American food, it's the restaurant's stunning location with views along the cliffs that overlook the Pacific Ocean.

San Francisco Zoo

1 Zoo Rd ⓣ415/753-7080, ⓦwww.sfzoo.org. Daily 10am–5pm. $10, free first Wed of each month. At the time of writing, the **San Francisco Zoo** is in the middle of a massive overhaul, set to conclude by the end of 2006 when all the old-fashioned enclosures will have been replaced with natural habitats; some are already open, including the Lemur Forest, a lush park home to a crowd of rare lemurs from Madagascar. The African savannah enclosure is scheduled to debut sometime in 2004, while the great apes' current concrete homes will be replaced by a massive forest two years after that. In the meantime, make sure to check out the new Children's Zoo, with its beautifully restored, old-fashioned Carousel ($2) and the charming Penguin Island, where the colony of chatty, highly sociable birds is fed every day at 3pm.

Shops

Andronico's Market

1200 Irving St at 14th ⓣ415/661-3220. California's gourmet answer to Safeway, with pricey but gorgeous produce that's great to grab for a picnic lunch in the park, plus microbrew beers and a fine wine selection.

Flat Plastic Sound

24 Clement St at 2nd ⓣ415/386-5095, ⓦwww.flatplasticsound.com. Vinyl specialist music store, offering both classical and obscure retro pop. The encyclopedic staff are especially attentive.

Green Apple

506 Clement St at 6th ⓣ415/387-2272, ⓦwww.greenapplebooks.com. Funky, browsable store with deft, eccentric touches like the regular sec-

tion of "Books that will never be Oprah's picks."

Le Video

1231 9th Ave at Irving ⓣ415/566-3606, ⓦwww.levideo.com. Two adjacent stores containing the most comprehensive collection of videos in the country, with both domestic and imported rarities.

Cafés

Cool Beans

4342 California St at 6th ⓣ415/750-1955. This brightly painted neighborhood coffeehouse is a charming hippie throwback with star- and flower-shaped tables, plus board games to play. There's the usual selection of sandwiches, cakes, and coffees.

▲ COOL BEANS

Louis

902 Point Lobos Ave ⓣ415/387-6330. Old-school diner near Cliff House, with brown formica tables and wide sea views – standard food, budget prices. Breakfast and lunch only.

Sweet Delite

519 Clement St at 6th ⓣ415/386-8222. First, gawp at the racks and racks of Chinese and American candies in plastic boxes here, then gorge on a bag of exotic sweets. There's also an ice cream bar that serves creamy, scented tapioca ball tea.

Wing Lee Bakery

503 Clement St at 6th ⓣ415/668-9481. No-nonsense Chinese dim sum store where there's little English spoken and you can gorge on pearlescent peanut dumplings for a couple of bucks.

Restaurants

Angkor Wat

4217 Geary Blvd at 6th ⓣ415/221-7887. The best Cambodian food in town – most of their tasty, cheap dishes involve basil, peanuts, or chiles, though the catfish with spicy lime sauce is also delicious. Famous for once having hosted the Pope for dinner.

Avenue 9

1243 9th Ave at Irving ⓣ415/664-6999. Southern-style food is served with panache at this mid-price eatery, where traditional dishes like baked chicken are spruced up California-style with swiss chard, arugula, and applewood bacon.

Mandalay

4348 California St at 5th ⓣ415/386-3895. Even if the decor at this budget Burmese restaurant is a little bland, the food is anything but – some of their more notable specials, scrawled on the chalkboard out front, include green papaya salad or remarkable homemade tofu dishes.

PJ's Oyster Bed

737 Irving St at 9th ⓣ415/566-7775, ⓦwww.pjsoysterbed.com Weekdays,

this rowdy, unpretentious restaurant offers spicy, tangy Cajun dishes such as blackened catfish for around $15–18; while on weekends it adds fish specials like a meaty Peruvian stew. Whatever the day, watch for the free vodka jello shots that the owner passes out.

Q

225 Clement St at 3rd ⓣ415/752-2298. This hipster outpost in the Richmond is an over-the-top diner, with funky features like a booth at the back where a tree grows through the table. Portions are huge, and the menu's mostly comfort food, like southern fried chicken or beer-battered catfish (each $9.50).

Rohan

3809 Geary Blvd at 2nd ⓣ415/221-5095, ⓦwww.rohanlounge.com. Funky lounge and bar, swathed in taffeta curtains, serving contemporary twists on Korean cuisine – grills are only $7.50–9.50 and *bi bam bap* $5.50 – until 1.30am at weekends.

The Russian Bear

939 Clement St at 8th ⓣ415/752-8197, ⓦwww.russianbear.citysearch.com. Russian restaurant popular with expats thanks to its traditional dishes like borscht and veal – the decor is mind-boggling, what with seemingly every surface mirrored or covered in gilt.

Tommy's

5929 Geary Blvd at 23rd ⓣ415/387-4747. Most people come for the enchiladas at this homey, low-cost Mexican restaurant. It's energetic and supercrowded whatever day or time, and is known for its exhaustive selection of obscure tequilas.

Bars

Bitter End

441 Clement St at 5th ⓣ415/221-9538. The youngest and hippest of the Irish bars on the main Richmond drag, notable for its cozy fireplace and impressive selection of whiskeys.

Pig & Whistle Pub

2801 Geary Blvd at Wood ⓣ415/885-4779. A thoroughly British pub, serving a good selection of English and Californian microbrews. There's a dartboard and jukebox crammed with Brit-rock classics.

Trad'r Sam's

6150 Geary Blvd at 26th ⓣ415/221-0773. Open since 1939, this is a classic Tiki bar, complete with flaming bowls of exotically named cocktails – try a P38 cocktail, served in a salad bowl with four straws.

▼ OCEAN BEACH

Performing arts and films

Four Star

2200 Clement St at 23rd ⓣ415/666-3488, ⓦwww.hkinsf.com. Funky Richmond theater screening a mix of art films and Hong Kong action flicks for the local Asian community.

Berkeley

A fifteen-minute BART ride brings you to the East Bay, home to two wildly different cities, Oakland (see p.153) and Berkeley. Notorious as a hippie haven and antiwar hotspot in the 1960s, Berkeley today retains the friendly, unflappable vibe that Haight-Ashbury has long lost. This is mostly due to the massive university that dominates the town – a fact underscored by the hordes of bobbing backpacks that fill its streets and cafés every weekday. But you don't have to be politically passionate to come here: this city was also where the light, ingredient-driven cooking style known as California cuisine was first invented. It's also a feast for readers – Telegraph Avenue, downtown's main shopping drag, is lined with bookstores, where you can easily spend an entire day browsing for hard-to-find first editions or trashy pulp paperbacks.

UCAL-Berkeley campus

Ⓣ510/642-5215, Ⓦwww.berkeley.edu. 90min tours Mon–Sat 10am, Sun 1pm. Free. Founded in 1873 on a former cow pasture by high-minded refugee academics from the East Coast, the university (as well as the city) was named to honor Irish bishop/philosopher/poet George Berkeley, whose lines "Westward the course of the empire takes its way" so inspired the founders. Its half-mile square main campus is so bucolic and tree-crammed that it looks like a forest onto which a university has been forcibly grafted, the large Neoclassical buildings jutting out suddenly from behind leafy copses. And despite such on-campus quirks as a café called the *Free Speech Movement Café*, the student body here is oddly normal-looking-when compared to the hippie stereotype Berkeley is often associated with.

If you choose not to take one of the chatty, free tours, the best walking route around the campus follows Strawberry Creek, the path running off southeast from the main entry on West Entrance Road. It leads through the greenery to Sproul Plaza, the campus's largest public space, usually lined with tables shilling student societies or the clink and bong of Hare Krishna converts.

Though the cynical might be tempted to sneer at the university's supposed idealism, it's impossible not to warm to the

▼ SATHER GATE AT BERKELEY

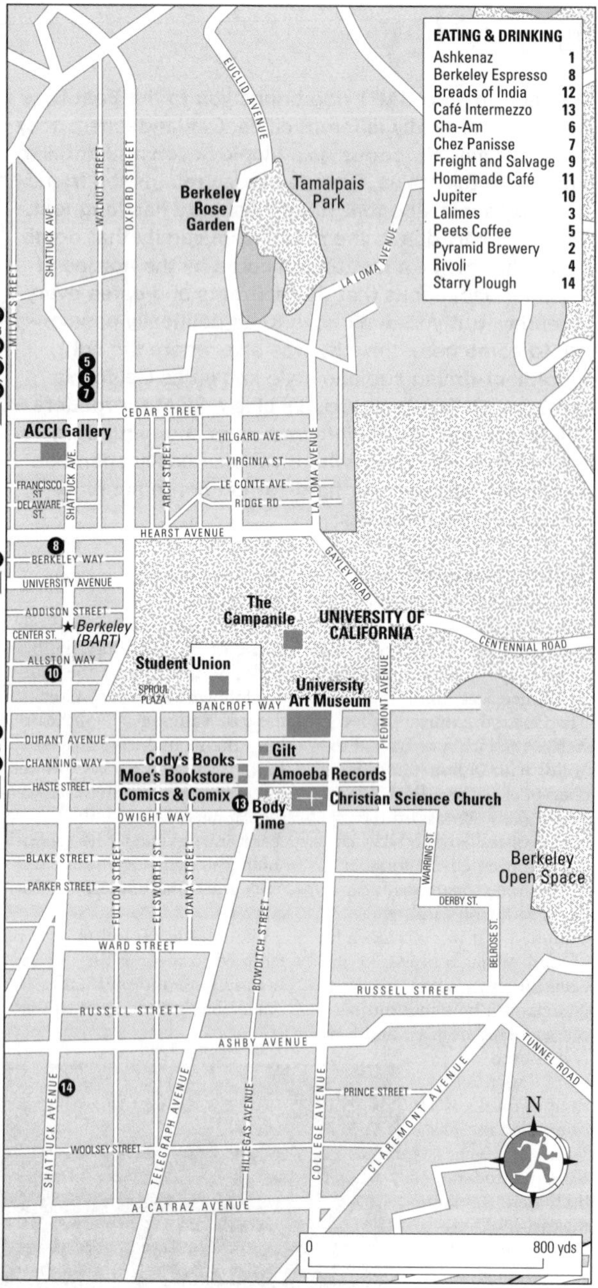

EATING & DRINKING

Ashkenaz	1
Berkeley Espresso	8
Breads of India	12
Café Intermezzo	13
Cha-Am	6
Chez Panisse	7
Freight and Salvage	9
Homemade Café	11
Jupiter	10
Lalimes	3
Peets Coffee	5
Pyramid Brewery	2
Rivoli	4
Starry Plough	14

1, 2, 3 & 4
9
11 & 12

Euclid Avenue
Tamalpais Park
Berkeley Rose Garden
La Loma Avenue
Shattuck Ave.
Walnut Street
Oxford Street
Milva Street
Cedar Street
ACCI Gallery
Hilgard Ave.
Virginia St.
Le Conte Ave.
Ridge Rd
Arch Street
La Loma Avenue
Francisco St
Delaware St.
Shattuck Ave.
Hearst Avenue
Berkeley Way
University Avenue
Gayley Road
Addison Street
Center St.
Berkeley (BART)
Allston Way
The Campanile
University of California
Centennial Road
Student Union
Sproul Plaza
Bancroft Way
University Art Museum
Piedmont Avenue
Durant Avenue
Channing Way
Haste Street
Gilt
Cody's Books
Moe's Bookstore
Amoeba Records
Comics & Comix
Body Time
Christian Science Church
Dwight Way
Warring St.
Berkeley Open Space
Blake Street
Parker Street
Fulton Street
Ellsworth St.
Dana Street
Derby St.
Bowditch Street
Belrose St.
Ward Street
Russell Street
Russell Street
Ashby Avenue
Tunnel Road
Shattuck Avenue
Telegraph Avenue
Hillegas Avenue
College Avenue
Prince Street
Claremont Avenue
N
Woolsey Street
Alcatraz Avenue
0
800 yds

place while walking around here; and it's worth remembering that the university's hippie reputation often obscures its superb scholarly record. This is where plutonium was discovered in 1941, and the element berkelium was first isolated by Berkeley-based boffins (hence the name). Just remember, if you want to sound like a local, don't shorthand to Berkeley – call it UC or Cal. The best way to explore is to wander around the campus, though we've picked out two highlights below: otherwise, another place to check out is the university's Botanical Garden (daily 9am–5pm, 7pm in summer; free) on the hillier, eastern edge of the campus, thirty lushly landscaped acres of cacti and plants.

▼ CAMPANILE

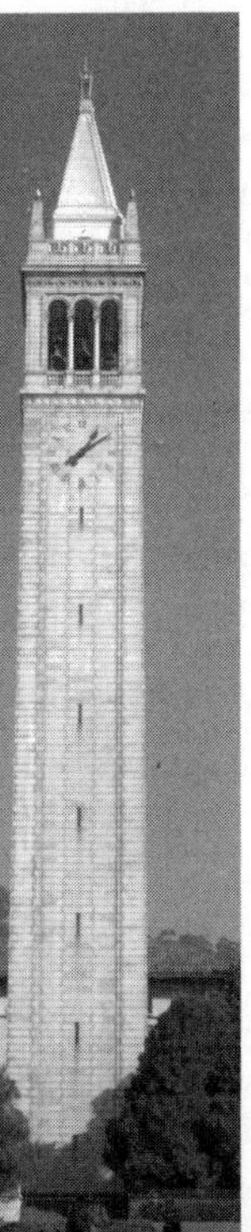

Campanile

Ⓣ510/642-5215, Ⓦwww.berkeley.edu/visitors/campanile.html. Mon–Fri 10am–4pm, last ride 3.45pm; $2. Like a monochrome replica of the clocktower in Venice's St Marks Square, the Sather Tower (its official name) was put up in 1917, using more than 500 tons of structural steel to crossbrace the building and secure it against tremors. It's poorly located at the rear of the campus, resulting in hit and miss views, especially if the Bay is fogbound – though on most days, you should be able to pick out the cone of the Transamerica Pyramid (see p.70); what's most surprising is how much less green and rural Berkeley's campus looks from on high. The less mobile should note that there's a long elevator ride then a narrow stairway to reach the top.

University Art Museum

2626 Bancroft Way at College Ⓣ510/642-0808, Ⓦwww.bampfa.berkeley.edu. Wed, Fri–Sun 11am–5pm, Thurs 11am–7pm; $8, free Thurs. A Modernist, angular building that stands out amid the twee Neoclassicism elsewhere on campus. The museum houses both a selection of European greatest hits from Picasso, Cézanne; and Rubens, as well as a stunning round-up of 1950s American favorite Hans Hofmann. There are almost fifty of his canvases here spanning Hofmann's entire career, from early figurative works like *Japanese Girl* to later, daubed abstracts such as *Indian Summer*. Check the museum's website for up-to-date info on their impressive and often controversial roster of traveling exhibits.

Telegraph Avenue

Telegraph Avenue is the commercial strip that services the campus's needs, filled with bargain sandwich stores and take-out restaurants plus record and book shops – the blocks running south of campus to Alcatraz Avenue are an especially bustling place to browse. It's appealing enough at any time, but only on a weekday lunchtime can you truly gauge how much the hordes of stu-

▲ PLAYING CHESS ON TELEGRAPH AVENUE

dents drive the surrounding town's economy.

Christian Science Church

2619 Dwight Way at Bowditch ⓣ510/845-7199. Built in the Craftsman style with a few Gothic touches, this handsome church looks like a collision of Swiss chalets, squished together to form a single building, their individual roofs jutting out in odd places from the final structure. The architect was Bernard Maybeck, the same man behind the mournful and equally detailed Palace of Fine Arts in the Presidio (see p.101). The church is laid out in a Greek Cross floor plan and spanned by a massive redwood truss, with carved neo-Gothic tracery and Byzantine-inspired painted decoration. The only public tours take place on the first Sunday of every month, starting at 12.15pm, but if you're in town at other times, you're always welcome to attend services (Sunday 11am, Wed 8pm).

Shops

Amoeba Records

2455 Telegraph Ave ⓣ510/549-1125, ⓦwww.amoebamusic.com. Though the branch in Haight-Ashbury is handier, this is the original site of the Bay Area's best second-hand record shop and it shows. The selection's bigger and the staff even nerdier, so you'll likely be able to find almost any CD you want, no matter how obscure it may be. It's also worth stopping by to pick up the flyers advertising cheap local gigs.

Body Time

2509 Telegraph Ave ⓣ510/548-3686, ⓦwww.bodytime.com. Although this Bay Area-born company sold its original name to the UK-based Body Shop, it still puts out a full range of aromatic natural bath oils, shampoos, and skin creams and offers soaps by the slice and custom-scented lotions.

Cody's Books

2454 Telegraph Ave ⓣ510/845-7852, ⓦwww.codysbooks.com. Acknowledged for its size and selection as the highest profile of the numerous local booksellers, specializing in fiction, poetry, and literary critcism.

Comics and Comix
2502 Telegraph Ave ⓣ510/845-4091. Sci-fi and comic heaven, heavy on figurines, current issues, and trinkets; smallish back issue stock.

Gilt
2391 Telegraph Ave ⓣ510/486-9699, ⓦwww.gilt.com. Handmade cosmetics, offering soaps by the slice like cheese, smelly candles, and decorative bath beads.

Moe's Bookstore
2476 Telegraph Ave ⓣ510/849-2087, ⓦwww.moesbooks.com. Vast four-story new and used bookstore, renowned for its art section on the top floor.

▲ BERNARD MAYBECK'S CHRISTIAN SCIENCE CHURCH

Cafés

Berkeley Espresso
1900 Shattuck Ave at Hearst ⓣ510/848-9576. Relaxed and less overrun by students than other cafés, this large, loungeable café, dotted with blond wood chairs and rickety tables, offers free wireless DSL and serious doorstep-sized sandwiches.

Café Intermezzo
2442 Telegraph Ave at Haste ⓣ510/849-4592. Come to this café for huge sandwiches on homemade bread (many of them $5 or less), plus great coffee and enormous salads, slathered in one of its house mixed dressings.

Homemade Café
2454 Sacramento St at Dwight Way ⓣ510/845-1940. If you want a hearty breakfast, there's nowhere better in town – though expect to share a table when at peak hours as it's a tiny space. There are some Jewish touches, like cheese blintzes, amongst the traditional offerings, as well as a few Mexican accents – the Home Fry Heaven smothers its potatoes in cheese, salsa, sour cream, and guacamole.

Peets Coffee
2124 Vine St at Walnut ⓣ510/841-0564, ⓦwww.peets.com. The cutesy West Coast chain of coffee houses started with this original branch, which opened in 1966.

Restaurants

Breads of India
2448 Sacramento St at Dwight ⓣ510/848-7684. Leave lots of room for the breads, a specialty at this tasty but cramped Indian lunch spot.

Cha-Am
1543 Shattuck Ave at Cedar ⓣ510/848-9664. Climb the stairs up to this always crowded budget restaurant, tucked away in the upscale Gourmet Ghetto, for deliciously spicy Thai food at bargain prices.

Chez Panisse

1517 Shattuck Ave at Cedar ⓣ510/548-5525, ⓦwww.chez-panisse.com. First and still the best of the modern Californian cuisineries, overseen by legendary chef Alice Waters. Dinner's served at two sittings, 6pm and 8.30pm, with a prix fixe menu that costs $50–75 depending on the night of the week. Some of the delights served here include Dungeness crab and petrale sole ravioli with chervil and chives and a Bosc pear cornmeal *crostata* with vin santo ice cream. Reservations essential.

Lalimes

1329 Gilman St at Peralta ⓣ510/527-9838, ⓦwww.lalimes.com. Unofficially known as "Chez Panisse for locals," this is another upscale gourmet outpost that offers an outstanding take on California cuisine in a low-key setting. The a la carte menu changes monthly, to allow for seasonal specials, though the *foie gras terrine* ($12.75) and chocolate torte ($6.25) are both sumptuous staples. Make sure to book well in advance – it's full every night of the week.

Rivoli

1539 Solano Ave at Peralta ⓣ510/526-2542, ⓦwww.rivolirestaurant.com. The atmosphere at this low-lit Mediterranean restaurant is casual but friendly. Though the intriguing menu (entrees run $18–22) changes every three weeks, three signature dishes always remain – a hot fudge sundae, a Caesar salad, and the true standout, tender portobello mushroom fritters with lemon aioli ($7.95).

Bars

Jupiter

2181 Shattuck Ave at Center ⓣ510/843-8277, ⓦwww.jupiterbeer.com. This bar has a multitude of beers, live jazz on weekends, and an outdoor beer garden. The decor has a distinctly German Gothic vibe, from seats made from church pews to the large chandeliers.

Pyramid Brewery

901 Gilman St at 8th ⓣ510/528-9880, ⓦwww.pyramidbrew.com. Great microbrewed beers – try the Hefeweizen – in a popular pub, a brightly lit, loft-style space with ample seating. There are tours of the on-site brewery daily at 4pm.

Starry Plough

3101 Shattuck Ave at Prince ⓣ510/841-2082, ⓦwww.starryplough-pub.com. Convivial Irish bar with bargain-price live rock and country many evenings and a handy dartboard.

Clubs and live music

Ashkenaz

1317 San Pablo Ave ⓣ510/525-5054, ⓦwww.ashkenaz.com. World music and dance café that presents acts ranging from modern Afrobeat to the best of the Balkans. Cover $5–10.

Freight and Salvage

1111 Addison St ⓣ510/548-1761, ⓦwww.thefreight.org. Founded in 1968, this coffeehouse-style venue is a nonprofit dedicated to preserving and promoting traditional music (whether blues, jazz, or folk) and its usual line-up leans heavily on singer-songwriters. Cover $15.50–23.50.

Oakland

Working-class and largely African-American, Oakland is often eclipsed by both San Francisco and Berkeley. The city's fiercest claim to fame lies more in its past association with radical political movements (it was the birthplace of the Black Panthers) and literary bigwigs (both Jack London and Gertrude Stein grew up here) than any current attractions. Despite the best regeneration efforts of charismatic mayor Jerry Brown, Oakland's compact downtown can still seem oddly lifeless outside office hours. The best reason to come is to see the prettified streets of Old Oakland, whose Victorian-era brick architecture showcases what San Francisco would look like today were it not for the tragedy of the 1906 earthquake and fire.

Chinatown

bounded by Broadway, Alice, 13th, and 7th streets. In comparison with San Francisco's bustling, throbbing Chinatown, the Oakland enclave is oddly empty of people: there are few trinket stores, and most of the shopfronts are filled with Vietnamese or Chinese supermarkets which spill fragrant produce onto the sidewalk. It's only during the last weekend of August that the streets really come to life, when the Chinatown StreetFest brings out performers, stalls, and the crowds.

▲ JACK LONDON STATUE

The Black Panthers

Formed amidst the poverty of West Oakland in 1966 by black-rights activists Huey Newton and Bobby Seale, the leather jacket- and beret-sporting members of the Black Panther Party for Self-Defense captured the media spotlight with their militant rhetoric and occasional gun battles with police.

Mixing socialism with black pride, the Panthers developed "survival programs" in black communities that included the establishment of free medical clinics. But infighting took a heavy toll, and when Newton fled to Cuba in 1974 to avoid prosecution for drug use, a cascading series of resignations led to the group's disbanding by the end of the decade. Former Panther David Hilliard conducts **Black Panther Legacy Tours** ($25; ⓣ510/986-0660, ⓦwww.blackpanthertours.com) through the Huey P. Newton Foundation on the last Saturday of each month. Tours depart at noon across from the main library on West 18 Street.

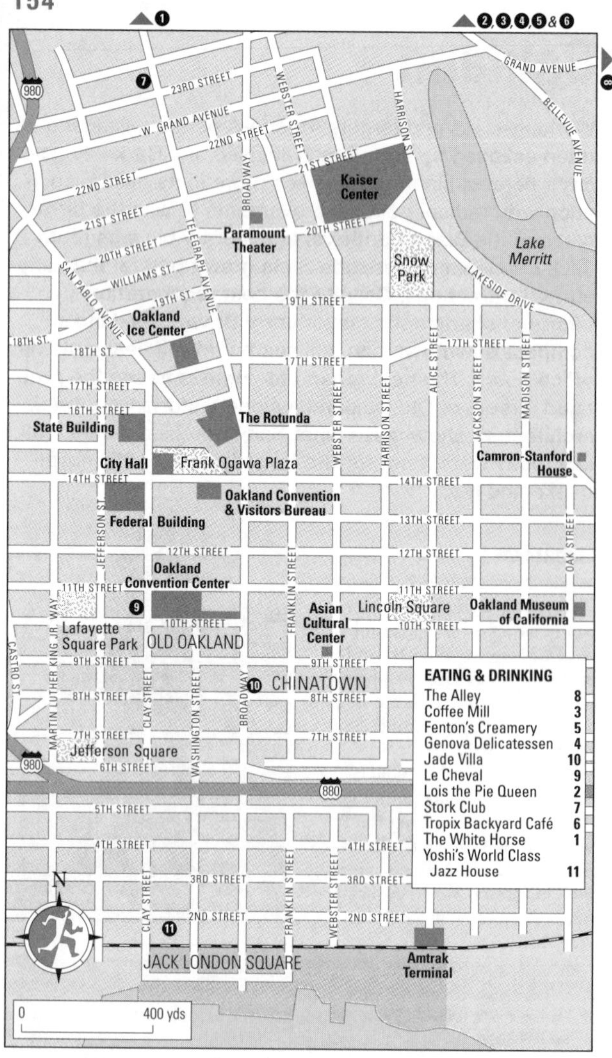

Old Oakland

bounded by Broadway, Clay, 11th, and 8th streets www.oldoakland.com. Dating back to the 1870s, this district holds a superb collection of grand old Victorian commercial architecture that's worth exploring even if modern restoration has left it feeling a little too manicured with uniform signage and flawless cream and gilt paintwork. Most of the storefronts are home to attorneys or interior design firms so there are few places to browse, though there's an excellent **Farmers Market** every Friday from 9am to 2pm. The liveliest area, filled with one-off stores and cafés, is at the corner of Washington and Eighth streets.

Jack London Square

Embarcadero and Broadway ⓣ510/814-6000, ⓦwww.jacklondonsquare.com. Named after hometown hero Jack London, this waterfront mall complex is anchored by a massive Barnes and Noble and filled with unremarkable brand-name eateries like *TGI Friday's* and *Tony Roma's*. Its only lures are its fine waterfront location, and the fact that there are fewer souvenir hawkers and less tourist tack than at Fisherman's Wharf. London completists should grab a pint at *Heinold's First and Last Chance Saloon*, a tiny slanting bar built in 1883 from the hull of a whaling ship where London actually drank – note the slanted door, that's never been fixed since it skewed in the wake of the 1906 earthquake. The other appealing draw here is *Yoshi's*, a first-rate jazz club.

Paramount Theatre

2025 Broadway at 20th ⓣ510/893-2300, ⓦwww.paramounttheatre.com. $1 tour, first and third Sat of each month at 10am. Though built by the same architect as the ornate, Mediterranean Revival Castro Theater (see p.126), this imposing landmark, with its Egyptian-inspired mosaic-clad facade, is a streamlined Art Deco masterpiece from 1931. It's worth trying to catch one of the infrequent tours of the building, or even stopping by for a movie (complete with Wurlitzer organ), so you can see the elaborate, mosaic- and relief-studded interior; the hodgepodge of styles is a result of the large number of artists hired to help decorate it. The Paramount also hosts live shows and stage spectaculars.

Oakland Museum of California

1000 Oak St at 10th ⓣ510/238-2200 or 1-888/625-6873, ⓦwww.museumca.org. Wed–Sat 10am–5pm, Sun noon–5pm, first Fri of each month 10am–9pm. $8, free second Sun of each month. This museum's housed in a stark and impressive modernist building designed by legendary architect Kevin Roche (one of the team behind the fabled TWA terminal at New York's JFK airport). Architectural value aside, the views across the city and the Bay from the rooftop sculpture garden are stunning. As for its holdings, they're smartly curated in three distinct sections, one per floor: California Ecology simulates the state's diverse climates from seaside to mountaintop, while California History ranges from early Native American settlement to the modern day. The best section, though, is undoubtedly the top floor, which showcases a collection of California arts, including some fine examples of turn-of-the-century Arts & Crafts furniture. The museum's currently undergoing a multimillion-dollar interior and exterior facelift, which should significantly enhance its exhibition space, due for completion in 2006.

▼ PARAMOUNT THEATRE

Cafés

Coffee Mill

3363 Grand Ave at Elwood ⓣ510/465-4224. This café doubles as an art gallery and often hosts poetry readings, too.

Fenton's Creamery

4226 Piedmont Ave at Ridgeway ⓣ510/658-7000, ⓦwww.fentonscreamery.com. The ultimate old-style ice cream parlor serving sundaes, sandwiches, fries, and snacks.

Genova Delicatessen

5095 Telegraph Ave at 51st ⓣ510/652-7401. Friendly deli, decked with hanging sausages, that serves chunky sandwiches for around $5.

Jade Villa

800 Broadway at 8th ⓣ510/839-1688. One of the best places to sample dim sum or Cantonese cuisine in Chinatown at fair prices.

Restaurants

Le Cheval

1007 Clay St at 10th ⓣ510/763-8495. A moderately priced Vietnamese restaurant, serving simple food in chic, spacious surroundings.

Lois the Pie Queen

851 60th St at Adeline ⓣ510/658-5616. Locally legendary for its Southern-style sweet potato pies, this cozy diner serves hearty breakfasts and dinners for less than $10.

▼ DOWNTOWN OAKLAND

Tropix Backyard Café

3814 Piedmont Ave at Yosemite ⓣ510/653-2444. Come to this cheerful café for their large portions of fruity Caribbean delicacies at reasonable prices, with authentic jerk sauce and thirst-quenching mango juice.

Bars

The Alley

3325 Grand Ave at Santa Clara ⓣ510/444-8505. A piano bar where locals come specifically to sing – given the boozy conviviality and the right melody, you will too. Closed Mon.

The White Horse

6551 Telegraph Ave at 66th ⓣ510/652-3820, ⓦwww.whitehorsebar.com. Oakland's oldest gay bar – a smallish, friendly place, with mixed dancing for men and women nightly.

Clubs and live music

Stork Club

2330 Telegraph Ave ⓣ510/444-6174, ⓦwww.storkcluboakland.com. On the main road toward the U-Cal Berkeley campus, this historic club is presently a favorite with DJs and indie bands. Closed Mon. Cover $5.

Yoshi's World Class Jazz House

in Jack London Square ⓣ510/238-9200, ⓦwww.yoshis.com. A combination jazz club and sushi bar that routinely attracts the biggest names in jazz. Cover $5–40.

Excursions

The land north of San Francisco is lush and rural; if you want to escape the city for a short time, this is the most worthwhile direction to head in. First up is the parkland of Marin County, a fine place for a bracing hike and also the closest site to San Francisco for anyone who wants to see the huge old redwoods that once covered the hillsides. Further on, the Wine Country of the Napa and Sonoma valleys is much quainter, studded with fine restaurants and wineries that produce America's most impressive vintages. Almost every one is open for tastings, but even teetotalers will enjoy the rolling countryside and ambling lifestyle.

▼ DRIVING ACROSS THE GOLDEN GATE BRIDGE

The Marin Headlands

Marin Headlands Information Center, alongside Rodeo Lagoon ☎415/331-1540, ⓦwww.nps.gov/goga/mahe/. Daily 9.30am–4.30pm. Coming to the undeveloped Marin Headlands, just across the Golden Gate from San Francisco, you'll find some of the most impressive views of the bridge and the city behind – at least if the fog holds off. The rugged landscape makes it a great place for an isolated clifftop scramble, especially among the ruins of old forts and gun emplacements that date from as recently as World War II back to the Civil War.

The park's best-designed hike is the Coastal Trail – also the best biking route – which begins at the northern end of Golden Gate Bridge and climbs the mountain facing back toward the city before plunging into Rodeo Valley to the west then looping back. If all that hiking's worn you out and you want to relax for a while, stop off at Rodeo Beach, a wide sandy strip that curls around Rodeo Lagoon, a warm, marshy area where swimming's sadly prohibited to protect the breeding seabirds.

Angel Island

Angel Island Visitor Center ☎415/435-1915, ⓦwww.angelisland.org or www.parks.ca.gov. Daily 9am–4pm. The largest island in the Bay –

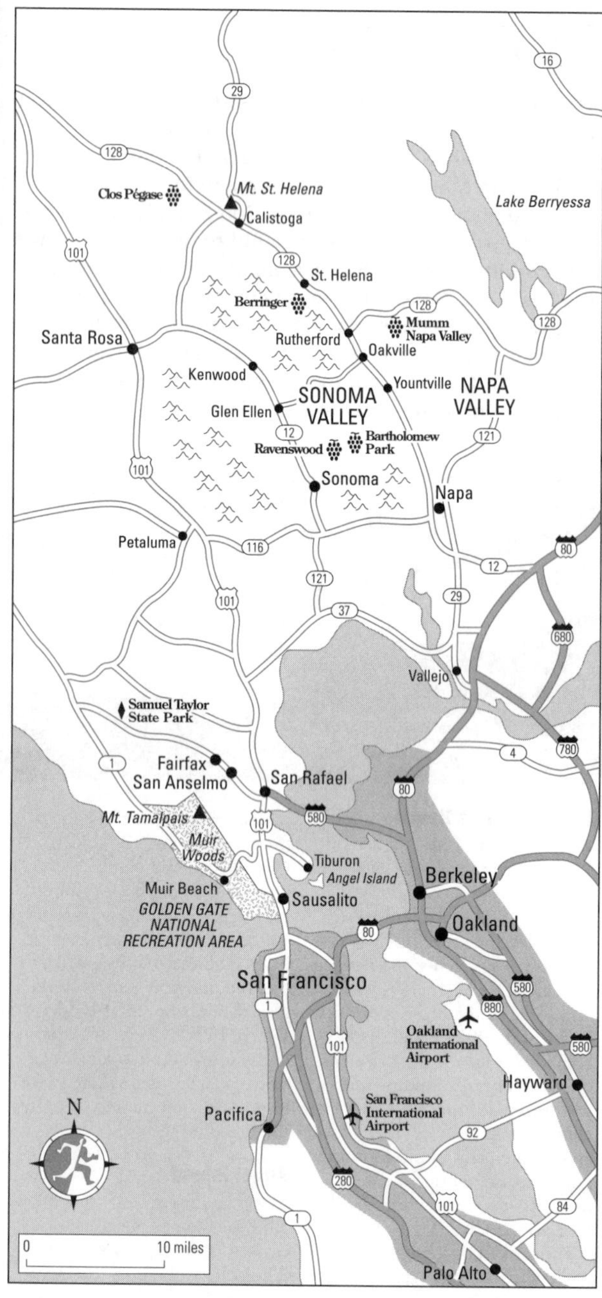

Mt. St. Helena
Clos Pégase
Calistoga
Lake Berryessa
St. Helena
Berringer
Mumm Napa Valley
Rutherford
Oakville
Santa Rosa
Kenwood
Yountville
SONOMA VALLEY
NAPA VALLEY
Glen Ellen
Bartholomew Park
Ravenswood
Sonoma
Napa
Petaluma
Vallejo
Samuel Taylor State Park
Fairfax
San Anselmo
San Rafael
Mt. Tamalpais
Muir Woods
Tiburon
Angel Island
Berkeley
Muir Beach
Sausalito
GOLDEN GATE NATIONAL RECREATION AREA
Oakland
San Francisco
Oakland International Airport
Hayward
San Francisco International Airport
Pacifica
N
Palo Alto
0
10 miles

it's ten times the size of Alcatraz – is also a state park, having served in the past as an immigration station and then a prisoner-of-war camp during World War II. As there are only a few ruins that mark the island's military past, the draw is mainly the greenery, with oak and eucalyptus trees covering the hills above rocky coves and sandy beaches. It's ideal for an energetic bike ride, especially up to the hump of **Mount Livermore**, which offers panoramic views of the Bay Area – you can rent bikes by the hour or day once you arrive ($10/hr or $30/day, ⓣ415/897-4715). As for beaches, the most appealing is **Quarry Beach**, a clean, sandy, and sheltered enclave protected from the bracing winds that whip through the Golden Gate. You can reach the island by boat from the Ferry Building downtown ($12 round trip, ⓣ415/705-5555, ⓦwww.blueandgoldfleet.com).

Sausalito

This pretty, smug little town, sitting directly north of San Francisco on the water, was once a gritty community of fishermen and sea traders, full of bars and bordellos. Now it's a cute (but self-consciously so) seaside town where there's little to do other than eat at one of the swanky restaurants, browse the pricey boutiques that line its picturesque waterfront promenade, or gawp at the expensive houses that loom from the overgrown cliffs above Bridgeway Avenue, the main road. The one sight that's really worth the detour is the bizarre but informative **Bay Model Visitor Center**, 2100 Bridgeway (Tues–Sat 9am–4pm; donation; ⓣ415/332-3870), where elevated walkways in a huge building lead you around a scale model of the entire Bay, simulating the changing tides and powerful currents. There's a regular **ferry service** across the Bay, operated by Blue and Gold Fleet from Pier 41 at Fisherman's Wharf ($7.25 each way; 6–7 trips daily; ⓣ415/705-8200; ⓦwww.blueandgoldfleet.com); it docks next to the Sausalito Yacht Club in the town center.

Mount Tamalpais Park

ⓣ415/388-2070, ⓦwww.cal-parks.ca.gov. Free. Daily 7am–sunset.

Mount Tamalpais (known by the less tongue-twisting nickname of Mount Tam) dominates the skyline of the Marin peninsula to the north and gives its name to the sprawling state park around it, where there are some thirty miles of hiking trails – where the mountain bike was first invented – not to mention stunning views across the Bay. To reach its impressive peak, head for the Pan Toll Ranger Station and continue up on the Pan Toll Road, which will drop you within a few hundred yards of the summit: hike up here and you'll be rewarded with breathtaking views of the distant Sierra Nevadas.

▼ SAUSALITO'S WATERFRONT

Muir Woods

☎415/388-2595, ⓦwww.visitmuirwoods.com. Daily 8am–sunset, $3. Named after a nineteenth-century naturalist, Muir Woods is home to 556 acres of redwood trees, most of which are more than 500 years old, and which once covered the whole area. Though Muir is a majestic and tranquil spot, where the sunlight filters three hundred feet down from the treetops to the laurel- and fern-covered canyon below, it's also a prime tour destination and is often clogged with coachloads on weekends. If you want to ditch the crowds, hike away from the paved paths that potter through the forest and start climbing on the steep trails that cling to the canyon's sides – if you look hard enough, you're likely to spot salamanders and newts in the damp undergrowth.

▼ MUIR WOODS

Napa Valley

As soon as you arrive in the Wine Country, it's easy to see why Napa and Sonoma valleys have been so romanticized, with their cool, oak tree-shaded ravines, mineral springs, and chaparral-covered ridges. The town of Napa itself is an expensive and unremarkable place; you're better heading past it to the spring town of Calistoga, which produces the namesake mineral water as well as hosting several curative spas. Oddly, despite its fame and the fact that vines have been tended here since missionary days, the Napa region doesn't produce much wine (only five percent of California's total output); but what it does churn out is far and away the best in the country so is well worth sampling. The 300 **wineries** here are all comfortably geared to handle hordes of visitors, but a few stand out, like **Mumm** and **Beringer**.

Dr Wilkinson's Hot Springs

1507 Lincoln Ave, Calistoga. ☎707/942-4102, ⓦwww.drwilkinson.com. Treatments start at $49. The best known of the area's hot springs is a health spa-cum-hotel (rates from $109) where you can enjoy heated mineral water treatments or volcanic ash tension-relieving massages.

Sonoma Valley

Smaller, more rustic, and more welcoming, Sonoma Valley is home to fewer wineries than Napa, but is also less choked with daytrippers; there are ambling backroads quilting the countryside here, and at least a fleeting sense of laid-back local life. Among the 45 or so vineyards, **Bartholomew** and **Ravenswood** especially merit visits. The most attractive town is Sonoma itself, filled with dozens of historic Mexican-era buildings, all dotted around a grassy downtown square. Historically, Sonoma's best known as the site of the Bear Flag Revolt in 1846, which propelled California into independence from Mexico and then into statehood. In the revolt, a few dozen angry Anglo settlers declared their independence here by hoisting a pennant with a bear on it that's the basis for the current state flag. Three weeks later, the United States declared war on Mexico and annexed California without firing a shot.

Wineries

Bartholomew Park Winery

1000 Vineyard Lane, Sonoma ⓣ707/935-9511, ⓦwww.bartholomewparkwinery.com. Self-guided tours of winery and tastings, daily 10am–4.30pm. Tours free, tasting $5. Bartholomew is housed in an enormous Spanish Colonial building and offers a museum of local history where there's an introduction to the rudimentary rules of winemaking. The real lure, though, is its affordable, drinkable wines – it's the best place to pick up a case or two to take home.

Beringer

2000 Main St, St Helena ⓣ707/963-7115, ⓦwww.beringer.com. Tasting tours daily 10am–5pm. $5. Beringer is home to the most famous piece of architecture in the area. The Rhine House was designed not in the prevailing Mission style but rather in the neo-Gothic tradition, modeled after the Beringer family estate back in Germany. Its wines are uniformly impressive, though the small selection of dessert vintages are standouts.

Mumm Napa Valley

8445 Silverado Trail, Rutherford ⓣ707/942-3434, ⓦwww.mummnapavalley.com. Free tours daily 10am–3pm, tastings daily 10am–5pm. $5–12. Co-owned by the French Champagne house, the Mumm vineyard produces fizzy and fresh sparkling wines – but it's also famous for its chatty, high-energy tours that avoid too much hard selling.

▲ THE REASON TO GO ON WINERY TOURS

Ravenswood

18701 Gehricke Rd, Sonoma ⓣ707/933-2332, ⓦwww.ravenswood-wine.com. Tours daily by reservation only at 10.30am, tasting room open 10am–4.30pm. $4. For pure unpretentious fun your best bet is Ravenswood, which lives up to its scrappy slogan, "No Wimpy Wines," by producing robust zinfandels and even hosting friendly barbecues in its tasting rooms during the summer.

Restaurants

Café Sarafornia

1413 Lincoln Ave, Calistoga ☎707/942-0555. This downhome diner is famous for its cheap, delicious breakfasts and lunches, not to mention its chatty owner. Expect a wait at the weekend.

The Coffee Garden

421 1st St W, Sonoma ☎707/996-6645. Fresh sandwiches are served on the back patio of this 150-year-old adobe café, where there's also a small (if unremarkable) gift shop on site too.

French Laundry

6640 Washington St, Yountville ☎707/944-2380, Ⓦwww.sterba.net/yountville/frenchlaundry/. Famed gourmet hotspot, arguably the best restaurant on the West Coast, and housed in a small stone building that serves outstanding Californian cuisine – you'll need to dress up (jackets, no jeans) and reserve a table two months in advance (call first thing in the morning too). There's a five-course prix fixe for $105, but true foodies should plan to splurge on the chef's tasting menu ($120), which sprawls over almost a dozen courses and usually features classics of French cuisine like *foie gras* and crème brulée.

La Casa

121 E Spain St, Sonoma ☎707/996-3406. Friendly, festive, and inexpensive Mexican restaurant just across from the Sonoma Mission – the enchiladas are especially tasty.

Ondine

558 Bridgeway, Sausalito ☎415/331-1133. This is a luxurious, expensive hotspot perched on the edge of Sausalito, with stunning views of San Francisco. But it's also appealing for the intriguing, fish-heavy fusion food, like a green papaya salad with Maine crab. Around $30 per entree.

Pinot Blanc

641 Main St, St Helena ☎707/963-6191, Ⓦwww.patinagroup.com. California fusion food at top-notch prices, in a romantic, if self-consciously rustic, setting. The wine list is impressive and almost exclusively Californian, as is the food – try the Sonoma duck breast with red rice ($22.95).

Poggio

801 Bridgeway, Sausalito ☎415/331-5888. A new Italian restaurant, with fine views across the Bay, serving Tuscan-inspired cuisine that emphasizes the lighter end of Italian cooking – try the petrale sole ($17). Lunch, when entrees run $6–13, is an inexpensive way to sample the menu.

Accommodation

Accommodation

Hotels

Hotels in San Francisco are plentiful, and there's a wide variety to choose from, but don't expect too many bargains: rooms will usually cost at least $100 per night. There's the usual raft of big-name hotels; but if you're looking for local charm, there's a cluster of boutique hotel groups, including Kimpton (Ⓦwww.kimptongroup.com), Joie de Vivre (Ⓦwww.jdvhospitality.com), and Personality (Ⓦwww.personality-hotels.com) that are a quirkier option – we've included our pick of their properties in the selections below. As for location, the densest concentration of rooms can be found around Union Square (including Chinatown and the Theater District) – this is a handy place to stay for public transit, and since there are so many rooms, you should be able to haggle during off-season since the cheaper hotels are gasping for business. If you're driving, it's easier and cheaper to stay further out, especially since parking, nightmarishly expensive downtown, is often included in the overnight rate at motels on the waterfront or in the city's western districts.

Union Square and the Theater District

Adagio 550 Geary St at Jones Ⓣ415/775-5000, Ⓦwww.jdvhospitality.com. The decor at this hotel echoes its ornate Spanish Revival facade with deep reds and ochres, and the large rooms are well appointed with all mod cons. The *Adagio* also provides free computers with high-speed Internet access and even free printing facilities. Rooms start at $119.

Clarion Hotel Cosmo 761 Post St at Jones Ⓣ415/673-6040 or 1-800/252-7466, Ⓦwww.hotel-cosmo.com. A high-rise hotel aiming for a funkier feel than most chains, with its lavender and lilac lobby and jaunty elevator music, though the white formica-filled rooms feel a little cheap. Try to snag a room on the upper floors so you can enjoy the views. Rates from $129.

Clift Hotel 495 Geary St at Taylor Ⓣ415/775-4700 or 1-800/658-5492, Ⓦwww.ianschragerhotels.com. The rooms at this Ian Schrager outpost are vaguely Asian and vintage Starck, with quirky touches like mirrored Louis XIV-style chairs. It's pricey, swish, and ultra-cool; just don't expect smiles from the staff. Note that the walls here are very thin, so bring earplugs. Rates start at $325.

Accommodation practicalities

The Visitor Information Center (see p.000) can provide the latest accommodation options, while San Francisco Reservations (Mon–Fri 6am–11pm, Sat–Sun 8am–11pm; Ⓣ510/628-4450 or 1-800/677-1500, Ⓦwww.hotelres.com) will find you a room from around $100 a double. British visitors can reserve rooms through Colby International (Mon–Fri 10am–5pm; Ⓣ0151/220 5848, Ⓦwww.colbyintl.com).

For B&Bs, contact a specialist agency such as Bed and Breakfast California (Ⓣ408/867-9662, Ⓦwww.bbintl.com) or Bed and Breakfast San Francisco (Mon–Fri 9am–5.30pm, Ⓣ415/899-0060, Ⓦwww.bbsf.com).

Rates in this chapter refer to the approximate cost of a double room throughout most of the year; be aware that rates will rise, sometimes significantly, at peak times. Bear in mind that for hotels, motels, and bed and breakfasts you will have to pay room tax – currently fourteen percent of the total bill – on top of these rates.

ACCOMMODATION
0
800 yds
N
Adagio 19
Argonaut 1
Baldwin 13
Best Western Carriage Inn 30
Best Western Tuscan Inn 2
Boheme 4
Clarion House Cosmo 16
Clift 23
Commodore International 15
Fairmont 8
Grant 12
Green Tortoise Hostel 6
HI-Union Square 24
Hotel Diva 20
Huntington 9
Mark Hopkins Inter-Continental 10
Monaco 22
Mosser 26
Pacific Tradewinds Guesthouse 7
Palace 21
Palomar 25
Phoenix 27
Prescott 17
Renoir 29
San Remo 3
SW Hotel 5
Triton 14
Westin St Francis 18
White Swan Inn 11
YMCA 28
FISHERMAN'S WHARF
The Cannery
TELEGRAPH HILL
Church of St. Peter & Paul
Coit Tower
Washington Square
NORTH BEACH
City Lights Bookstore
Columbus Tower
CHINATOWN
Cablecar Museum
PORTSMOUTH SQUARE
Transamerica Pyramid
Grace Cathedral
Bank of America
Chinatown Gate
THEATER DISTRICT
Union Square
TENDERLOIN
Museum of Modern Art
Yerba Buena Gardens
Moscone Convention Center
CIVIC CENTER
Civic Plaza
San Francisco Public Library
Main Post Office
SOMA
JEFFERSON STREET
BEACH STREET
NORTH POINT ST.
BAY STREET
FRANCISCO STREET
CHESTNUT STREET
LOMBARD ST.
GREENWICH ST.
FILBERT STREET
UNION STREET
GREEN STREET
BROADWAY
PACIFIC AVENUE
JACKSON ST.
WASHINGTON STREET
WASHINGTON ST.
CLAY STREET
SACRAMENTO STREET
CALIFORNIA STREET
PINE STREET
BUSH STREET
SUTTER STREET
POST STREET
GEARY ST.
O'FARRELL ST.
ELLIS ST.
EDDY ST.
TURK ST.
MCALLISTER ST.
THE EMBARCADERO
MASON ST.
POWELL ST.
STOCKTON ST.
KEARNY ST.
COLUMBUS AVENUE
TAYLOR STREET
MASON STREET
GRANT AVE.
MONTGOMERY STREET
SANSOME STREET
LEAVENWORTH STREET
POWELL STREET
STOCKTON STREET
GRANT AVENUE
KEARNY STREET
LARKIN STREET
HYDE STREET
JONES STREET
MARKET STREET
STEVENSON ST.
JESSIE ST.
MARY ST.
FIFTH STREET
SIXTH ST.
FOURTH STREET
THIRD STREET
TEHAMA ST.
CLEMENTINA ST.
FOLSOM STREET
SHIPLEY STREET
CLARA STREET

Commodore International 825 Sutter St at Jones, ⓣ415/923-6800 or 1-800/338-6848, ⓦwww.thecommodorehotel.com. Rooms here are decorated in warm, earthy colors, offset by shiny steel neo-Deco fixtures; the refurbished bathrooms are blindingly white and clean. Though the decorations don't vary, each room is named after a local attraction like the Haas Lilienthal House or the Mission murals. Rooms from $75.

Hotel Diva 440 Geary St at Taylor ⓣ415/885-0200 or 1-800/553-1900, ⓦwww.hoteldiva.com. The sleek, steel lobby at this boutique hotel echoes the rooms, which are large and minimalist, with brushed metal furniture and huge, comfy beds. Rates $169 and up.

Monaco 501 Geary St at Taylor ⓣ415/292-0100 or 1-800/214-4220, ⓦwww.monaco-sf.com. A quirky boutique hotel housed in a historic Beaux Arts building that features canopied beds in each highly colored, rather overwrought room. It's known for providing complimentary goldfish to keep lonely travelers company in their rooms. Rooms from $169.

Prescott 545 Post St at Mason ⓣ415/563-0303, ⓦwww.prescotthotel.com. Sumptuous and opulent hotel with large rooms decorated in warm woods and rich colors. Service is flawless – attentive and polite – and the amenities offered with concierge-level rooms, like free breakfast and evening drinks, make the splurge worthwhile. Rates from $245.

Westin St Francis 335 Powell St at Sutter ⓣ415/397-7000 or 1-800/WESTIN1, ⓦwww.westin.com. This landmark's sumptuous lobby features the *Westin*'s unofficial mascot, a grand grandfather clock, ornate ceiling, and a gauche painting of Queen Elizabeth. It's been the site of many scandals over the years – including the attempted assassination of Gerald Ford – but frankly, the rooms are disappointingly plain after such a riotous entrance. Rooms start at $199.

Chinatown

Baldwin 321 Grant Ave at Bush ⓣ415/781-2220 or 1-800/6-BALDWIN, ⓦwww.baldwinhotel.com. Surprisingly quiet, given this hotel's hub location in the heart of Chinatown, with simply furnished, neutral-colored rooms. Rates are negotiable off-season and generally begin at $89.

Grant 753 Bush St at Mason ⓣ415/421-7540 or 1-800/522-0979, ⓦwww.granthotel.citysearch.com. A good value considering its central location, this hotel has small but clean rooms, overpowered a little by the relentlessly maroon carpets. Basic but convenient. Rooms from $50.

Triton 342 Grant Ave at Bush ⓣ415/394-0500 or 1-888/364-2622, ⓦwww.hotel-tritonsf.com. Trippy, eccentric hotel that offers modern amenities like a 24hr gym and in-room fax as well as weirder services like nightly Tarot card readings. The rooms themselves are stylish but gaudy. Rooms from $189.

North Beach

Boheme 444 Columbus Ave at Vallejo ⓣ415/433-9111, ⓦwww.hotelboheme.com. A smallish hotel with tiny but dramatic rooms featuring canopied beds and Art Deco-ish bathrooms decked out in rich, dark colors. Ask for a room at the back if you're a light sleeper. Rates begin at $164.

San Remo 2237 Mason St at Chestnut ⓣ415/776-8688 or 1-800/352-7366, ⓦwww.sanremohotel.com. Known for its chatty, helpful staff, this warren-like converted house has cozy, chintzy rooms, all of which share spotless bathrooms. Note that there are no phones or TVs in the bedrooms and no elevator, but the low prices still make it a bargain. Rooms from $50.

SW Hotel 615 Broadway at Grant ⓣ415/362-2999, ⓦwww.swhotelsf.com. This well-located hotel has rooms decorated in modern Asian style, with carved armoires and headboards, plus bright yellow bedspreads. Rates start at $119.

Nob Hill

Fairmont 950 Mason St at Sacramento ⓣ415/772-5000 or 1-800/441-1414, ⓦwww.fairmont.com. Most famous of the city's top-notch hotels, this gaudy palace has four restaurants and lounges, as well as fantastic views from the rooms, which are luxurious but unexciting. Don't miss the *Tonga Room* bar (see p.92) in the basement. Rates start at $269.

Huntington 1075 California St at Taylor ⓣ415/474-5400, ⓦwww.huntingtonhotel.com. Bogart and Bacall lived for several years at this landmark hotel, which has elegant (in an old-money sort of way) common areas and large if unexciting rooms, many of which have kitchenettes. Rooms from $250.

Mark Hopkins Inter-Continental 1 Nob Hill, 999 California St at Mason ⓣ415/392-3434, ⓦwww.interconti.com. A grand, castle-like hotel that was once the chic choice of writers and movie stars but is now more corporate in design and atmosphere. Rooms are decorated in a vaguely Art Deco style, heavy on creams and blacks – though all are identical, prices rise as the floors do. The hotel's also home to the *Top of the Mark* bar (see p.92). Rates start at $355.

Fisherman's Wharf

Argonaut 495 Jefferson St at Hyde ⓣ415-397-5572 or 1-800/790-1415, ⓦwww.argonauthotel.com. This brand-new nautical-themed hotel (there's an anchor motif running through much of the decoration) in the Cannery complex has large, lush rooms that feature DVD players, stereos, and impressive views. Surprisingly quiet for its location. Rooms start at $349.

Best Western Tuscan Inn 425 North Point at Mason ⓣ415/561-1100 or 1-800/648-4626, ⓦwww.tuscaninn.com. Despite its name, this waterfront hotel is more English country manor than Tuscan farmhouse, with cozy rooms decorated in warm colors. It has attentive touches like an afternoon wine reception and a free limo to downtown in the mornings. Rooms $189 and up.

Pacific Heights and Cow Hollow

Hotel Del Sol 3100 Webster St at Lombard ⓣ415/921-5520 or 1-877/433-5765, ⓦwww.jdvhospitality.com. The best place for budget cool in the city, this funky mosaic-wrapped motor lodge has a tropical theme, as well as a swimming pool, all done out in zesty colors; ditto the basic but bright rooms. Rates $99 and up.

Hotel Drisco 2901 Pacific Ave at Broderick ⓣ415/346-2880 or 1-800/634-7277, ⓦwww.hoteldrisco.com. A super-luxurious hotel at the peak of Pacific Heights with spectacular city views and attentive, unobtrusive service. Overall it feels more like a country B&B than a hotel, thanks to the parlor-like common areas. There are VCRs in every room and complimentary sherry every afternoon. Rates from $175.

Queen Anne 1590 Sutter St at Octavia ⓣ415/441-2828 or 1-800/227-3970, ⓦwww.queenanne.com. Gloriously overdone restored Victorian (it began as a girls' school before becoming a bordello) where each room is stuffed with gold-accented Rococo furniture and bunches of silk flowers. The late Miss Mary Lake, former principal of the school, is said to still make periodic supernatural appearances in room 410. Rooms from $139.

Surf Motel 2265 Lombard St at Pierce ⓣ415/922-1950. This old-school motel has two tiers of bright, simple rooms that are sparklingly clean. Be sure to ask for a room at the back to escape the noise from the street. Rates start at $59.

SoMa

Best Western Carriage Inn 140 7th St at Mission ⓣ415/552-8600. The enormous, elegant rooms with sofas and working fireplaces, plus free breakfast, come close to making up for the location on a slightly sketchy block. Rates begin at $139.

The Mosser 54 4th St at Market ⓣ415/986-4400, ⓦwww.victorianhotel.com. A cool recent conversion that fuses Victorian touches like ornamental molding with mod leather sofas. Though the chocolate- and olive-colored rooms are tiny, each is artfully crammed with amenities, including multi-disc CD players. Rooms from $99.

Palace 2 New Montgomery St at Market ⓣ415/512-1111, ⓦwww.sfpalace.com. Hushed, opulent building, well known for its famous Garden Court tearoom (a favorite of presidents and heads of state); though you'll enjoy the cache of staying here, the gold and green English country house-style rooms are small for the sky-high prices. Rates $249 and up.

Palomar 12 4th St at Market ⓣ415/348-1111 or 1-877/294-9711, ⓦwww.hotel-palomar.com. Chic, neo-Nouveau bolthole, with a dark and smoky color scheme, plus ebony and leopard-print accents; the rooms are pleasantly large and packed with amenities, even fax machines. Rooms from $229.

Tenderloin and Civic Center

The Phoenix 601 Eddy St at Larkin ⓣ415/776-1380 or 1-800/248-9466, ⓦwww.thephoenixhotel.com. This raucous, retro motel conversion is a favorite with up-and-coming bands when they're in town. There's a small pool, and the 44 rooms are eclectically decorated in tropical colors with changing local artwork on the walls. Rates start at $99.

The Renoir 45 McAllister St at 7th ⓣ415/626-5200 or 1-800/576-3388, ⓦwww.renoirhotel.com. This hotel's location in a wedge-shaped building overlooking Market Street makes it especially popular during Gay Pride for the views along the parade route. The rooms have recently been florally, if unexcitingly, refurbished. Rooms from $119.

The Castro

Beck's Motor Lodge 2222 Market St at Sanchez ⓣ415/621-8212 or 1-800/227-4360. The clientele here is more mixed than you'd expect from its Castro location, and the soft, bluish rooms are plusher than the gaudy yellow motel exterior might suggest. Rooms from $89.

Haight-Ashbury and around

Hayes Valley Inn 417 Gough St at Hayes ⓣ415/431-9131 or 1-800/930-7999, ⓦwww.hayesvalleyinn.com. This secluded inn has homey, apple-green rooms with a well-stocked kitchen/breakfast nook that's a great place to meet people. Note that bathrooms are all shared. Rooms from $52.

Stanyan Park 750 Stanyan St at Waller ⓣ415/751-1000, ⓦwww.stanyanpark.com. A small, neat hotel overlooking Golden Gate Park – its sumptuous, heavily draped rooms with four posters are oddly incongruous in its counter-culture neighborhood. Rooms from $130.

The Richmond and the Sunset

Ocean Park Motel 2690 46th Ave at Wawona ⓣ415/566-7020, ⓦwww.oceanparkmotel.citysearch.com. San Francisco's first Art Deco motel is an outstanding example of Streamline Moderne architecture. It's also convenient for the beach and the zoo, plus there's a kids' play area. Rooms from $75.

Oceanview Motel 4340 Judah St at LaPlaya ⓣ415/661-2300, ⓦwww.oceanviewmotel.citysearch.com. No-frills lodging out in the Sunset District, with smallish, simply furnished rooms. There's free on-site parking and convenient Muni access. Rates start at $65.

Bed and breakfasts

San Francisco is filled with fancy B&Bs, most of them housed in historic buildings – in fact, staying at a B&B is an easy way to see the interior of a fully restored Victorian up close. Be aware, though, that you'll often be opting for the charms of a home-cooked breakfast, in exchange for sharing a shower. And if you're set on staying in Haight-Ashbury or the Castro, B&Bs are really the only choice, since large hotels have yet to invade those areas. Expect rates to start around $85, higher in summer; all will usually include a hearty breakfast and afternoon tea and sherry; we've noted, where applicable, the premium some charge for a private bathroom.

24 Henry 24 Henry St at Sanchez, Castro ⓣ415/864-5686 or 1-800/900-5686, ⓦwww.24henry.com. Tucked away on a leafy residential street, this small B&B is a predominantly gay male guest-house with five simple rooms, only one with private bath. $85 and up.

Archbishop's Mansion 1000 Fulton St at Steiner, Alamo Square ⓣ415/563-7872 or 1-800/543-5820, ⓦwww.thearch-bishopsmansion.com. The last word in camp elegance, this B&B hotel stands on the corner of Alamo Square and is crammed with $1 million worth of antiques, including the chandelier from *Gone with the Wind*. Each of the grand rooms is named after a different Italian opera – the largest (and priciest) is Don Giovanni. Rooms begin at $110.

The Carl 198 Carl St at Stanyan, Haight-Ashbury ⓣ415/661-5679 or 1-888/661-5679, ⓦwww.carlhotel.citysearch.com. A plain B&B that's a bargain for its Golden Gate Park location; it has small but pretty floral-decorated rooms that have microwaves and fridges; the six with shared bath are especially well priced. From $75 (private) or $55 (shared).

Dolores Park Inn 3641 17th St at Dolores, the Mission ⓣ415/621-0482, ⓦwww.doloresparkinn.net. Housed in an artfully restored Italianate Victorian, there are only four rooms at this sumptuous B&B; all are large and crammed with a baroque assortment of ornate European antiques. Rooms start at $129 including breakfast.

Inn on Castro 321 Castro St at Market, Castro ⓣ415/861-0321, ⓦwww.innon-castro2.com. Luxurious B&B that's spread across two nearby houses, with eight rooms and three apartments available, all of which are brightly decorated in individual styles and have private baths and phones. Rates start at $105.

The Red Victorian Bed, Breakfast and Art 1665 Haight St at Cole, Haight-Ashbury ⓣ415/864-1978, ⓦwww.red-vic.com. Bizarre B&B and "Peace Center," decorated with the owner's ethnic arts, where rooms vary from simple to opulent. Breakfast's a lavish but concertedly communal affair, so be prepared to chat with your neighbors while you eat. Most rooms share common baths. Rates start at $86.

White Swan Inn 845 Bush St at Mason, Union Square ⓣ415/775-1755 or 1-800/999-9570, ⓦwww.foursisters.com/inns/whiteswaninn. Top-tier B&B with a serious English manor theme, what with all the roaring fireplaces, oak-paneled rooms, and afternoon tea. Rooms from $185.

Hostels

San Francisco's hostels are first-rate and exceptionally good value for the amenities on offer – from free Internet terminals to curfew-free, 24-hour access. All the ones we've listed below are spotless and friendly, with a liberal, laid-back vibe and a welcoming staff. At most hostels, whether privately run or part of the HI network, a dorm bed will cost around $20, but since space is tight downtown and all these places are wildly popular, make sure to book ahead in high season. In each account, we've noted the specific amenities that are included in the price.

Green Tortoise 494 Broadway at Montgomery, North Beach ⓣ415/834-1000 or 1-800/867-8647. Laid-back hostel with dorm beds and double rooms (with shared bath). Extras include free Internet access, use of the small on-site sauna, complimentary breakfast, and there's no curfew. $19–22 dorms, $48–56 rooms.

HI-San Francisco Fort Mason Building 240, Fort Mason ⓣ415/771-7277, ⓦwww.hiayh.org or www.norcalhostels.org. This is a choice budget option for an outdoorsy traveler, a standard hostel on the waterfront in a park close to Fisherman's Wharf and housed in a historic Civil War-era barracks. It doesn't require a membership fee so it's even cheaper than hostels elsewhere; dorm beds cost $22.

HI-San Francisco Union Square 312 Mason St at Geary ⓣ415/788-5604, ⓦwww.norcalhostels.org. This hostel's four-person dorms are spotless, sharing bathroom facilities between eight people, while private rooms are pricier and sleep two; it's open 24 hours and there's a kitchen with microwave. Reservations recommended. Dorms $22/$25; private rooms $60/$66 (prices for members/non-members).

Pacific Tradewinds Guesthouse 680 Sacramento St at Kearny, Chinatown ⓣ415/433-7970 or (May–Oct) 1-800/486-7975, ⓦwww.sanfrancisco-hostel.com. The best budget option in the center of town, this small hostel offers free high-speed Internet access and a clean kitchen, plus a large, communal dining table that's an easy way to get to know fellow travelers. $17/person.

YMCA Central Branch 220 Golden Gate Ave at Leavenworth ⓣ415/885-0460, ⓦwww.centralymcasf.org. Simple rooms, but a great deal nonetheless – $12 overnight parking, free breakfast, and free use of YMCA fitness center. There are private rooms with bath as well as a few dorms. $23.50 dorm, $73.56 room (prices include tax).

Essentials

Essentials

Arrival

Unless you're coming from nearby on the West Coast, the quickest way to get to San Francisco is by flying. There are plenty of routes in by bus, and trains run to neighboring Oakland.

By air

All international and most domestic flights arrive at **San Francisco International Airport**, or **SFO** (Ⓣ1-800/435-9736 or 650/821-8211, Ⓦwww.flysfo.com), located about fifteen miles south of the city.

There are several ways of getting into town from here, each of which is clearly signed from the baggage claim areas. Most people take minibus shuttles into the city – companies include **Supershuttle** and **American Airporter**: the vans depart every five minutes from the center island on the road outside the departures level, and will take passengers to any city-center destination for around $12 a head; in light traffic, bank on a thirty-minute journey, but allow more time at rush hour. Be ruthless when negotiating prices – competition for these and the several other companies running shuttle services is fierce and lines nonexistent. The **SFO Airporter** bus is slightly cheaper ($10) and makes pick-ups outside each baggage claim area every fifteen minutes; the snag is that it only serves major hotels downtown.

The much-anticipated $1.5 billion **BART train line** from the airport to downtown has finally opened and is an efficient, slightly cheaper option: the ride takes thirty minutes and costs $4.70 (Ⓦwww.bart.gov). **Taxis** from the airport cost $25–30 (plus tip) for any downtown location – definitely worth it if you're in a group or too tired to care.

By train and bus

All of San Francisco's **Greyhound** services use the **Transbay Terminal** at 425 Mission St at 1st, SoMa (Ⓣ1-800/231-2222, Ⓦwww.greyhound.com). To connect from here to the BART network, walk one block north to the Embarcadero station on Market Street.

All **Amtrak trains** stop in Oakland (Ⓣ1-800/USA-RAIL or 209/832-8350, Ⓦwww.amtrak.com): there's daily service to here from up and down the West Coast, as well as from Denver and Chicago. Free shuttle buses run from the Oakland station across the Bay Bridge to the Transbay Terminal, or you can take BART into town – the Lake Merritt stop is a few blocks' walk northeast of here. A more efficient route is to get off Amtrak at Richmond to the north, where you can easily pick up BART nearby at the Richmond station.

By car

If you're **driving** into town from the east, the main route is **I-80**, which runs via Sacramento all the way from Chicago. I-5, fifty miles east of San Francisco, serves as the main north-south route, connecting Los Angeles with Seattle; the I-580 spur from I-5 takes you to the Bay area. Picking up a car at the airport, head for Hwy-101 North. Stay on this road until you hit the city.

Information

The outstanding **San Francisco Visitor Information Center** is on the lower level of Hallidie Plaza at the end of the cable car line on Market Street (Mon–Fri 9am–5pm, Sat & Sun 9am–3pm, closed Sun Nov–May; Ⓣ415/283-0177 or recorded information line Ⓣ415/283-0177, Ⓦwww.sfvisitor.org). There are free maps of the city as well as pamphlets on hotels and restaurants. The center also sells the **City Pass** ($33.25; Ⓦwww.citypass.net), a half-price ticket valid for entry to several key museums including SFMOMA and the Palace of the Legion of Honor, passage on a Blue and Gold Fleet San Francisco Bay cruise, plus a free week's pass on Muni transit.

For information about **what's on**, try the Sunday edition of the *San Francisco Chronicle* newspaper (50¢; Ⓦwww.sfgate.com); it includes a section known as the *Datebook* (also known as the "Pink Pages") which has previews and reviews for the coming week. Otherwise, pick up one of the two terrific **weekly freesheets**: *The Bay Guardian* (Ⓦwww.sfbg.com) and *SF Weekly* (Ⓦwww.sfweekly.com), available from racks around town, both of which offer more in-depth features on local life and better music and club listings than the *Chronicle*. As for local magazines, the free, monthly *PaperCity* is a fine source for trendier types; *San Francisco* magazine ($3.95; Ⓦwww.sanfran.com) is the long-established, rather toothless local glossy, while *7x7* is its upstart, slightly more exciting rival ($4; Ⓦwww.7x7mag.com). Both are often available free in hotels.

Useful websites

Citysearch Ⓦwww.sanfrancisco.citysearch.com. This megasite is a great place to track down a phone number or check a map; be careful, though, as some listings and reviews are out of date.

Craigs' List Ⓦwww.craigslist.org. The definitive community website started in San Francisco – locals swear by it. A fantastic resource for everything from jobs to concert tickets.

San Francisco Arts Ⓦwww.sfarts.org. Comprehensive listings of all things arty – you can search by date and discipline (dance, theater, music) to find exactly what you're looking for.

San Francisco Magazine Ⓦwww.sanfran.com. Online version of the local glossy. The magazine's features are fun and sometimes informative; but what's best about this site is its restaurant search engine.

SF Raves Ⓦwww.sfraves.org. Insider guide to nightlife with underground listings for clubs that are edgy and on the mark.

SF Station Ⓦwww.sfstation.com. Arguably the best local listings site – opinionated, up-to-date, and easy to use.

City transportation

San Francisco is one of those rare American cities where you don't need a car to see everything: in fact, given the chronic shortage of parking downtown, horrible traffic, and zealous traffic wardens, it makes more sense to avoid driving entirely. The **public transportation** system covers every neighborhood and is inexpensive, to boot. If you have stout legs to tackle those hills, consider **cycling** – but, frankly, **walking** the city is still the best bet (though even walkers should note that the steep gradients, especially around Nob Hill, can turn what looks like a five-minute walk on a map into a huffing, puffing fifteen-minute climb). If you have questions on any form of public transit in the Bay area call Ⓣ415/817-1717 or 673-MUNI or log on to Ⓦwww.transitinfo.org.

Muni

Muni (Ⓣ415/673-6864, Ⓦwww.sfmuni.com) is a comprehensive network of buses, trolley buses, and cable cars. Aside from buses and three picturesque cable car routes, there are five tram lines (see box opposite) which run underground along **Market Street** and above ground elsewhere, plus the old-style F tram that shuttles along **Market Street**, connecting the Embarcadero and the Castro.

On buses and trains the **flat fare** (correct change only) is $1.25; with

Muni tram lines

Muni F–Market Line Restored vintage trolleys from around the world run downtown from the Transbay Terminal up Market Street and into the heart of the Castro. The new extension along the refurbished Embarcadero to Fisherman's Wharf is one of Muni's most popular routes.
Muni J–Church Line From downtown to the Mission and the edge of the Castro.
Muni K–Ingleside Line From downtown through the Castro to Balboa Park.
Muni L–Taraval Line West from downtown through the Sunset to the zoo and Ocean Beach.
Muni M–Ocean View West from downtown by the Stonestown Galleria shopping center and San Francisco State University.
Muni N–Judah Line From the CalTrain station, past Pac Bell stadium to Downtown and west through the Inner Sunset to Ocean Beach.

each ticket you buy, ask for a free **transfer** – they're good for another two rides on a train or bus in any direction within ninety minutes to two hours of purchase. Note that cable cars cost $3 one-way and do not accept transfers. If you're in town for a while, the best option is to buy a Muni **passport pass**, available in one-day, three-day, and seven-day denominations ($9, $15, $20), which is valid for unlimited travel on the Muni system and BART trains (see below) within the city limits.

BART

Along Market Street downtown, Muni shares station concourses with **BART** (Bay Area Rapid Transit; ⓣ510/465-BART or 415/817-1717, ⓦwww.bart.gov), which is the fastest way to get to downtown Oakland and Berkeley, not to mention the Mission district. **Tickets** aren't cheap ($1.10–4.70, depending on how far you ride) but the service is efficient and dependable; trains follow four routes (which differ mostly only by their East Bay terminus) in a fixed schedule, usually arriving every ten minutes; save your ticket after entering the station as it is also needed when exiting the train. To **buy a ticket**, insert cash into the automated machine then use the buttons to reduce the amount by $1 or 5 cents until the appropriate value's reached; then press the print button, and pick up both your ticket and change at the same time.

Taxis

Flagging a **taxi** in San Francisco can be difficult – try hanging around the entrance of one of the larger hotels. Phoning around, try Veterans (ⓣ415/552-1300) or Yellow Cab (ⓣ415/626-2345, ⓦwww.yellocabsf.com). **Fares** (within the city) begin with a fee of $1.70 to start the meter and $1.80 per mile thereafter, plus the customary fifteen-percent tip.

Driving

The only reason to **rent a car** in San Francisco is if you want to explore the larger Bay area, the Wine Country, or north or south along the coast (for car rental info, see p.181). If you have to drive in town, pay attention to San Francisco's attempts to control downtown traffic: the posted speed limit is 30mph and pedestrians waiting in a crosswalk always have the right-of-way. In addition, it's almost impossible to make a left turn anywhere in downtown, meaning you'll have to get used to looping the block, making three rights instead of one left. Another challenge is **parking** – there's barely any on-street space, but you'll find plenty of garages – expect to pay $2.50 per fifteen minutes. If you do find a curbside space, note if the curb is painted any kaleidoscopically colored stripes, especially green (ten-minute limit for all vehicles), and yellow, yellow/black, yellow/green/black (no stopping for private vehicles). Also make sure to observe the

San Francisco law of curbing wheels on steep streets – turn wheels into the curb if the car points downhill and away from the curb if it points up.

Cycling

Cycling is a fantastic way to experience San Francisco. Golden Gate Park, the Marina and Presidio, and Ocean Beach all have great, paved trails and some off-road routes. Throughout the city, marked bike routes – with lanes – direct riders to all major points of interest, but note that officials picked the routes for their lack of car traffic, not for the easiest ride. If you get tired, bikes can be carried on most trains and an increasing number of buses. Blazing Saddles **bike store** has several locations (Ⓣ415/202-8888, Ⓦwww.blazingsaddlessanfrancisco.com or Ⓦwww.bikethebridge.com) – two of the most convenient are 1095 Columbus Ave at Francisco, North Beach and Pier 41. Rental for bikes is $7/hr, $28/day.

City tours

As you'd expect from a city as visitor-friendly as San Francisco, there are plenty of **tours** available to suit most any interest. Undoubtedly the most impressive (and expensive) option comes from San Francisco Helicopter Tours (Ⓣ1-800/400-2404 or 650/635-4500, Ⓦwww.sfhelicoptertours.com), who provide a variety of spectacular **flights** over the Bay area. Prices start at $20 per passenger for a twenty-minute flight.

There are plenty of **walking tours** available, but one of the best is City Guides (Ⓣ415/557-4266, Ⓦwww.sfcityguides.org), a terrific free series sponsored by each neighborhood's public library, which also includes themed walks on topics from the Gold Rush to the Beat Generation. Cruisin' the Castro Ⓣ415/550-8110, Ⓦwww.webcastro.com/castrotour) is the Grand Dame of San Francisco walks, in which Ms Trevor Hailey leads you through her beloved neighborhood, offering as much a history lesson as a sightseeing tour ($40, including brunch). A fun alternative is Wok Wiz Tours (daily 10am Ⓣ415/981-8989, Ⓦwww.wokwiz.com), a stroll through Chinatown run by chef-writer Shirley Fong-Torres and her team ($28, $40 including lunch).

For **boat cruises** around the Bay, check out Blue and Gold Fleet (Ⓣ415/773-1188, Ⓦwww.blueandgold-fleet.com), which offers chilly 75-minute trips with breathtaking views of the bay, leaving from piers 39 and 41 at Fisherman's Wharf – though be warned that everything may be shrouded in fog, making the price less than worth it ($20).

Many of the **bus tours** are unremarkable, but there are a couple of quirky standouts, for which reservations are essential: El Camión Mexicano (Ⓣ415/546-3747, Ⓦwww.mexican-bus.com) takes evening tours through the Mission on a surprisingly fun itinerary that takes in local Mexican restaurants and salsa clubs for drinking and dancing ($38). Three Babes and a Bus (Ⓣ1-800/414-0158, Ⓦwww.threebabes.com) is a whistlestop nightlife tour every Saturday at 9.30pm that's popular with bachelorette parties ($35). It's hugely cheesy but infectious fun.

Money

With an **ATM card** (and PIN number) you'll have access to cash from machines all over San Francisco, though as anywhere, you may be charged a fee for using a different bank's ATM network. To find the location of the nearest Bay area ATM, call: Amex ⓣ1-800/CASH-NOW, Plus ⓣ1-800/843-7587, or Cirrus ⓣ1-800/424-7787.

Most **banks** in San Francisco are open Monday–Friday 9am–3pm and a few are also open on Saturday 9am–noon. For banking services – particularly currency exhange – outside normal business hours and on weekends, try major hotels: the rate won't be as good, but it's the best option in a tight financial corner.

Phones, mail, and email

Greater San Francisco has a single **area code** – ⓣ415, and calls within this code are treated as local, while you'll be charged higher rates for the Wine Country (ⓣ707) or the East Bay (ⓣ510).

International visitors who want to use their **mobile phones** will need to check with their phone provider whether it will work in the US and what the call charges are; from elsewhere in the US, your phone should operate fine, but you may incur roaming charges. To call home internationally: dial 011 + country code + number, minus the initial 0. Country codes are as follows: Australia (61), Canada (1), New Zealand (64), UK & Northern Ireland (44), and Eire (353).

As for **mail**, international letters will usually take about a week to reach their destination; rates are currently 80¢ for letters and 70¢ for postcards to Europe or Australia. To find a post office, or check up-to-date rates, see ⓦwww.usps.com or call ⓣ1-800/275-8777.

If you need to check your **email** while in town (and didn't bring your laptop), you won't have a hard time doing so – especially as San Francisco's consistently topped polls of Most Wired City in the US. Expect to pay around $7/hr at most Internet cafés. If money's tight, head to the public library, where there's free fifteen-minute access for all – you'll have to sign up in advance, and expect a wait.

Festivals and holidays

San Francisco has a huge variety of special **festivals**, the biggest of which are detailed below. Remember that during some of these events, especially Pride, hotels and hostels will book up quickly so make sure to arrange accommodation well in advance. On the national **public holidays** listed in the box below, stores, banks, and public and federal offices are liable to be closed all day.

Chinese New Year

End of January or early February, depending on the lunar calendar ⓣ415/982-3000, ⓦwww.chineseparade.com. Chinatown's even livelier than

Public holidays

January
1: New Year's Day
3rd Monday: Dr Martin Luther King Jr's Birthday

February
3rd Monday: President's Day

May
Last Monday: Memorial Day

July
4: Independence Day

September
1st Monday: Labor Day

October
2nd Monday: Columbus Day

November
11: Veterans' Day
4th Thursday: Thanksgiving Day

December
25: Christmas Day

usual during this week-long celebration, which culminates in the Golden Dragon Parade when hundreds of people march through downtown leading a 75-foot-long dragon.

Cherry Blossom Festival

Late April ⓣ415/563-2313, ⓦwww.nccbs.org. For two consecutive weekends, Japantown's concrete is transformed into a rowdy celebration of all things Japanee. Highlights include a parade from Civic Center with floats and performers and, best of all, the beauty contest to choose the Queen of the festival.

Cinco de Mayo

The weekend nearest to May 5 ⓣ415/826-1401. Commemorating the Mexican victory at the battle of Puebla, this is a two-day party in the Mission – raucous, booze-filled, and great fun. The festival is in Civic Center Plaza while the parade runs down Mission Street between 24th and 14th streets.

Bay to Breakers Footrace

Third Sun in May ⓣ415/359-2800. Kooky, campy, and unique, this event nominally involves a 12km footrace beginning at Howard and Spear streets and ending at the ocean (kickoff at 8am), though it's really just another excuse for San Franciscans to go costume-crazy. Most of the 70,000 runners will be sporting outlandish costumes (or even running naked); an unmissable sight if you're in town.

San Francisco LGBT Pride Celebration Parade

Late June ⓣ415/864-5733, ⓦwww.sfpride.org. At one of the bigger and more boisterous Gay Pride events in the world, crowds of up to a half-million pack Market Street for an enormous party-cum-parade, then migrate across to City Hall for a giant block party, with outdoor discos, live bands, and numerous craft and food stands.

Halloween

October 31 ⓣ415/826-1401. Hundreds strut their stuff in this wild, over-the-top parade: though local powers-that-be have been pushing the procession into Civic Center for logistical reasons, the heart and soul of stuff-strutting is certainly still the Castro.

Directory

AMERICAN EXPRESS 455 Market St at First, Financial District ⓣ415/536-2600; Mon–Fri 9am–5.30pm, Sat 10am–2pm. Also at 311 9th Ave at Clement, Richmond ⓣ415/221-6760; Mon–Fri 9am–5pm.
CAR RENTAL Alamo ⓣ1-800/522-9696, ⓦwww.alamo.com. Avis ⓣ1-800/331-1084, ⓦwww.avis.com. Budget ⓣ1-800/527-0700, ⓦwww.budgetrentacar.com. Thrifty ⓣ1-800/367-2277, ⓦwww.thrifty.com.
CIGARETTES AND SMOKING Cigarettes are banned in all public indoor spaces (and generally frowned upon everywhere else), but are still available in virtually any food store, drugstore, or bar. While many local pubs turn a blind eye to patrons lighting up, be aware that if you're spotted by a beat cop patrolling the neighborhood, you and the bartender can each be given a $75 fine. Some bars – via a complex legal loophole – have managed to preserve a smoking section for puffing patrons: we've noted them in the text.
CONSULATES UK, 1 Sansome St at Market, Financial District (Mon–Fri 8.30am–5pm; ⓣ415/617-1300); Ireland, 100 Pine St at Front, Financial District (Mon–Fri 10am–noon, 2–3.30pm; ⓣ415/392-4214); Australia, 625 Market St at Montgomery, Financial District (Mon–Fri 8.45am–1pm, 2–4.45pm; ⓣ415/536-1970); New Zealand, One Maritime Plaza, Suite 400, Embarcadero (appointment only; ⓣ415/399-1255); Germany, 1960 Jackson St at Gough, Pacific Heights (Mon–Fri 9am–noon; ⓣ415/353-0300).
DISABLED ACCESS Unsurprisingly, all public buildings in San Francisco, including hotels and restaurants, are required to have wheelchair-accessible bathrooms and entrances, while Muni offers kneeling buses – for full listings, check ⓦwww.accessnca.com. The only place you could hit trouble is on the steep hills, especially Nob and Telegraph.
DRUGSTORES Walgreens 24hr pharmacies: 498 Castro St at 18th, Castro ⓣ415/861-6276; 3201 Divisadero St at Lombard, Marina ⓣ415/931-6415.
ELECTRICITY 110V AC.
EMERGENCIES ⓣ911.
OPENING HOURS Most museums will be open six or seven days a week, from at least 10am to 5pm, while stores will close at 6 or 7pm Mon–Sat, and slightly early on Sunday. As for restaurants, most will be busiest from 6–7.30pm, and many will stop serving dinner after 9.30pm.
HOSPITALS San Francisco General Hospital, 1001 Potrero Ave at 23rd, Potrero Hill (ⓣ415/206-8000 or 206-8111 for emergency); also has a 24hr emergency walk-in service and rape treatment center (ⓣ415/821-3222). Castro-Mission Health Center, 3850 17th St at Prosper, Mission (ⓣ415/487-7500); offers a drop-in medical service with charges on a sliding scale depending on income, plus free contraception and pregnancy testing. California Pacific (formerly Davies) Medical Center, Castro and Duboce, Lower Haight (ⓣ415/565-6060); 24hr emergency care and a doctors' referral service.
PASSPORT AND VISA OFFICE US Department of Immigration, 630 Sansome St at Washington, Jackson Square ⓣ1-800/375-5283.
POST OFFICE The main post office is at 101 Hyde St at Fulton, Civic Center (Mon–Fri 8.30am–5.30pm, Sat 10am–2pm; ⓣ1-800/275-8777. Other branches include Sutter Street Station, 150 Sutter St at Montgomery, Financial District (Mon–Fri 8.30am–5pm), and Rincon Finance Station, 180 Steuart St at Mission, SoMa (Mon–Fri 7am–6pm, Sat 9am–2pm).
RELIGIOUS SERVICES Grace Cathedral on Nob Hill at 1051 Taylor St has an Episcopalian (Anglican) congregation (ⓣ415/749-6300, ⓦwww.gracecathedral.org), while Catholics can worship at St Mary's Cathedral, 600 California St at Grant (ⓣ415/288-3800, ⓦwww.oldsaintmarys.org). The grandest synagogue is Congregation Emanu-El, 2 Lake St at Arguello Blvd, at the eastern edge of the Richmond district by the Presidio (ⓣ415/751-2535).

TAX Sales tax of 8.5 percent is added to virtually everything you buy in a store – except food – but isn't part of the marked price. Hotel tax will add 14 percent onto your bill.

TIME ZONE The West Coast runs on Pacific Standard Time (PST), always three hours behind the East Coast and eight hours behind the UK.

Index and small print

A Rough Guide to Rough Guides

San Francisco DIRECTIONS is published by Rough Guides. The first *Rough Guide to Greece*, published in 1982, was a student scheme that became a publishing phenomenon. The immediate success of the book – with numerous reprints and a Thomas Cook prize shortlisting – spawned a series that rapidly covered dozens of destinations. Rough Guides had a ready market among low-budget backpackers, but soon also acquired a much broader and older readership that relished Rough Guides' wit and inquisitiveness as much as their enthusiastic, critical approach. Everyone wants value for money, but not at any price. Rough Guides soon began supplementing the "rougher" information about hostels and low-budget listings with the kind of detail on restaurants and quality hotels that independent-minded visitors on any budget might expect, whether on business in New York or trekking in Thailand. These days the guides offer recommendations from shoestring to luxury and a large number of destinations around the globe, including almost every country in the Americas and Europe, more than half of Africa and most of Asia and Australasia. Rough Guides now publish:

- Travel guides to more than 200 worldwide destinations
- Dictionary phrasebooks to 22 major languages
- Maps printed on rip-proof and waterproof Polyart™ paper
- Music guides running the gamut from Opera to Elvis
- Reference books on topics as diverse as the Weather and Shakespeare
- World Music CDs in association with World Music Network

Visit **www.roughguides.com** to see our latest publications.

Publishing Information

This 1st edition published May 2004 by **Rough Guides Ltd**, 80 Strand, London WC2R 0RL.
345 Hudson St, 4th Floor, New York, NY 10014, USA.

Distributed by the Penguin Group
Penguin Books Ltd, 80 Strand, London WC2R 0RL
Penguin Group (USA), 375 Hudson Street, NY 10014, USA
Penguin Group (Australia), 487 Maroondah Highway, PO Box 257, Ringwood, Victoria 3134, Australia
Penguin Group (Canada), 10 Alcorn Avenue, Toronto, Ontario, Canada M4V 1E4
Penguin Group (NZ), 182–190 Wairau Road, Auckland 10, New Zealand
Typeset in Bembo and Helvetica to an original design by Henry Iles.
Printed and bound in Italy by Graphicom

192pp includes index
A catalogue record for this book is available from the British Library

ISBN 1-84353-318-9

1 3 5 7 9 8 6 4 2

Help us update

We've gone to a lot of effort to ensure that the first edition of **San Francisco DIRECTIONS** is accurate and up-to-date. However, things change – places get "discovered," opening hours are notoriously fickle, restaurants and rooms raise prices or lower standards. If you feel we've got it wrong or left something out, we'd like to know, and if you can remember the address, the price, the time, the phone number, so much the better.

We'll credit all contributions, and send a copy of the next edition (or any other DIRECTIONS guide or Rough Guide if you prefer) for the best letters. Everyone who writes to us and isn't already a subscriber will receive a copy of our full-color thrice-yearly newsletter. Please mark letters: "**San Francisco DIRECTIONS Update**" and send to: Rough Guides, 80 Strand, London WC2R 0RL, or Rough Guides, 4th Floor, 345 Hudson St, New York, NY 10014. Or send an email to **mail@roughguides.com**

Have your questions answered and tell others about your trip at **www.roughguides.atinfopop.com**

Rough Guide credits

Text editors: Chris Barsanti
Layout: Dan May
Photography: Nelson Hancock
Cartography: Melissa Baker
Picture research: Jj Luck
Proofreader: Margaret Doyle
Production: John McKay
Design: Henry Iles

The author

Mark Ellwood moved to America from England in 1998 and has lived out of a suitcase ever since, zigzagging from Washington State to Washington DC: on the way, among other things, he's learnt how to make shoo-fly pie and visited an all-psychic town. Mark is co-author of several other Rough Guides, including Miami and California, and also writes regularly on fashion and travel for various magazines.

Acknowledgments

Thanks to readers including Julie Stagg, A Lane, V Kyth, and Lee Robinson for their contributions to this new book. On a personal note, thanks to Letizia Treves for everything – whether company on a chilly early morning trip to Alcatraz or that midnight trek round the Mission's latest nightspots. Thanks also to Rachel Brown for first discovering San Francisco with me; to Alison Diboll for never refusing another glass of wine; to Virginia Cartwright and her irresistible affection for her adoptive city; to Laurie Armstrong and Tanya Pampalone at the CVB for their unstinting helpfulness; and to Rob Delameter, Wendy Downing and Tom Walton.Thanks as ever to Maureen, Karen and Ben for keeping the home fires burning in New York.

Photo credits

All images © Rough Guides except the following:

p.5 North Beach © Phil Schermeister/CORBIS
p.5 Lombard © Ron Stroud/Masterfile
p.6 Painted Ladies © Ron Stroud/Masterfile
p.7 Coit Tower From Russian Hill © Robert Holmes/CORBIS
p.7 Castro Theatre © Robert Holmes/CORBIS
p.8 Street scene © Ron Stroud/Masterfile
p.11 Aerial view of Alcatraz © Golden Gate National Recreation Area, National Park Service
p.13 Strybing Arboretum © Bruce Peters/California Horticultral Society
p.15 Washington Square Park © Morton Beebe/CORBIS
p.17 Queen Anne Hotel © Queen Anne Hotel
p.17 Archbishop's Mansion © Russell Abrahams
p.17 Clift Hotel © www.ianschragerhotels.com
p.19 Folsom Street © Fred R. McMullen
p.19 Neon lights on the Castro Theatre © Catherine Karnow/CORBIS
p.19 Armistead Maupin © Harrison David/CORBIS SYGMA
p.21 Oui, Three Queens © Evan Kaminsky
p.25 Church of St Peter & Paul © Saints Peter and Paul Church
p.28 Cherry Blossom Festival © Richard Cummins/CORBIS
p.28 Halloween on the Castro © Ed Kashi/CORBIS
p.29 Chinese New Year © Corbett Lee Photography
p.29 Cinco de Mayo Dancers © Morton Beebe/CORBIS
p.29 Gay Pride © Rick Gerharter
p.33 The Redwood Room, Clift Hotel © www.ianschragerhotels.com
p.34 SF Symphony © Terrence McCarthy
p.35 Theater Artaud © Robert Holmes/CORBIS
p.36 Mecca © Mecca
p.37 Home, The Castro © Home
p.37 Foreign Cinema, The Mission © Jeremy Mende
p.37 EOS © EOS
p.40 The Globe restaurant © The Globe
p.41 Chinatown Nightmarket © SanFranciscoChinatown.com
p.43 City Guides Walking Tour © Bryan F. Peterson/CORBIS
p.43 Sunday gospel services at Glide Memorial Church © Kevin Fleming/CORBIS
p.45 Gary Danko restaurant © Gary Danko Restaurant
p.45 Greens restaurant © Greens Restaurant
p.45 Chez Panisse © Clarissa Horowitz
p.46 SF Giants game © Deanne Fitzmaurice/San Francisco Chronicle/CORBIS
p.46 Biking around the Presidio © www.brendatharp.com
p.47 Rollerblading in Golden Gate Park © Ted Streshinsky/CORBIS
p.53 Fortune cookie © Royalty-Free/CORBIS
p.53 Topless Waitressing © Kim Kulish/CORBIS
p.57 Bay to Breakers Race © Bettmann/CORBIS
p.57 Good Vibrations © 2004 Good Vibrations, photo by Phyllis Christopher (www.phyllischristopher.com)

p.59 Campanile, UCAL-Berkeley © Mark E. Gibson/CORBIS

p.59 View of city from Alcatraz © Golden Gate National Recreation Area, National Park Service

p.87 Coit Tower From Filbert Steps © Robert Holmes/CORBIS

p.89 Lombard Street © Ron Watts/CORBIS

p.91 Mark Hopkins Inter-Continental © Karen Huntt Mason/CORBIS

p.103 Coastal homes along the Bay © Catherine Karnow/CORBIS

p.105 The Presidio © Morton Beebe/CORBIS

p.112 Yerba Buena park © S Grandadam/Robert Harding

p.136 Painted Ladies © Richard Cummins/CORBIS

p.159 Floating homes, Sausalito © S Grandadam/Robert Harding

p.161 Wine glass © Royalty-free/CORBIS

Last full page: Houses at Pacific Heights © J. A. Kraulis/Masterfile

Index

a

b

c

d

e

f

g

h

i

j

k

l

m

n

o

p

q

r

s

t

u

v

w

y

z